# FOR
# MINECRAFTERS

D1048245

# HACKS
# FOR
# MINECRAFTERS

## THE UNOFFICIAL GUIDE TO TIPS AND TRICKS THAT OTHER GUIDES WON'T TEACH YOU

MEGAN MILLER

Sky Pony Press
New York

Copyright © 2014 by Hollan Publishing, Inc.

Minecraft® is a registered trademark of Notch Development AB

The Minecraft game is copyright © Mojang AB

Sky Pony Press books may be purchased in bulk at special discounts for sales promotion, corporate gifts, fund-raising, or educational purposes. Special editions can also be created to specifications. For details, contact the Special Sales Department, Sky Pony Press, 307 West 36th Street, 11th Floor, New York, NY 10018 or info@skyhorsepublishing.com.

Sky Pony® is a registered trademark of Skyhorse Publishing, Inc.®, a Delaware corporation.

Minecraft® is a registered trademark of Notch Development AB.
The Minecraft game is copyright © Mojang AB.

Visit our website at www.skyponypress.com.

10 9 8 7 6 5 4 3 2

Library of Congress Cataloging-in-Publication Data is available on file.

Book design by Sara Kitchen

Print ISBN: 978-1-5107-3802-7
Ebook ISBN: 978-1-5107-4388-5

# TABLE OF CONTENTS

# INTRODUCTION

**Y**ou're a miner! You've mined for diamonds, killed a couple or a million zombies, and know not to dig straight up or straight down! Now what? Plenty. Minecraft is a constantly evolving sandbox game. This means the developers of the game add new things each year and there are many ways to play. For version 1.12, also known as the World of Color Update, Minecraft added colorful concrete and concrete powder blocks, patterned glazed terracotta blocks, a variety of parrots, the Illusioner illager, colored beds, and more! You can expect this game to grow and change as you learn, so there are always new things to explore and experiment with.

And each year, thousands of players find new tricks to get things done better, faster, or with more fun. This book will show you lots of ways to help your game, whether you like to fight zombies or build castles, including:

- how to save a village from a siege of zombies
- what to do first to defeat the Ender Dragon
- how to find one of your world's strongholds
- how to make automatic sliding doors using pistons and redstone
- how to move between Creative and Survival modes using cheats

**NOTE:** The tips in this book are based on Minecraft 1.12, Java (PC) edition, so if you are playing a different version or are playing on a console, you may find that some features work a little differently.

# CHAPTER 1

## PLAYING YOUR WAY

**M**inecraft is a sandbox game, which means there aren't any rules for how you play. In a sandbox, you can build a sandcastle, dig a road, or throw a bunch of sand around. In Minecraft, you can build a massive railway system, make friends with wolves and ocelots, explore the oceans, or kill an army of zombies. Or do it all. There's no goal that you must achieve, but if you like goals, Minecraft has a few you can set your sights on. It's up to you to decide how to play, and you can mix it up any way you want to.

## Minecraft Game Modes

Minecraft has different game modes you choose at the start. They are geared to the different types of gameplay.

- **Survival and Hardcore:** In Survival mode you have to find food and shelter, and you can be killed. If you are killed, you respawn at your starting point without your inventory. (Your inventory items stay at your death scene for five minutes before they despawn—so you do have a chance to get them back.) There are four difficulty levels: Peaceful (no mobs), Easy (mobs do less damage), Normal (mobs do normal damage), and Hard (mobs do more damage and you can die from hunger). In Hardcore mode, you play at Hard difficulty, and you can't have cheats. If you are killed, you can choose between respawning in Spectator mode or having your world completely deleted.

In Hard difficulty, mobs are more likely to spawn with weapons, armor, and enchantments, and they will cause you more damage.

- **Adventure:** Adventure mode is like Survival, except you can't interact with many blocks. It is designed for playing on adventure maps.

- **Creative:** Creative mode is perfect for building. You can fly around, and you have access to all the blocks. Your inventory changes to an item selection screen with a search page.

- **Spectator:** In Spectator mode, you can't touch or do anything, but you can fly all around the world and straight through blocks!

- **Changing Mode:** To change game mode while you are playing, create your world with cheats on. Then, to change mode, open the chat window by pressing T and type the following:

- [ ]  For Survival mode: /gamemode 0 (or /gamemode s or /gamemode survival)
- [ ]  For Creative mode: /gamemode 1 (or /gamemode c or/gamemode creative)
- [ ]  For Adventure mode: /gamemode 2, (or /gamemode a or /gamemode adventure)
- [ ]  For Spectator mode: /gamemode 3 (or /gamemode sp or /gamemode spectator)

In Creative mode you can fly around, which is a huge help if you're building a tower in sky!

## Want Some Goals?

If you are goal-oriented, you can play that way, too. Minecraft has a series of about forty advancements you can use as quests. Accomplish one and make your way to the next. These can also guide you through the Minecraft survival skills. They start off very simple, and you have probably already accomplished many. You can open the Advancements screen by pressing Escape and then Advancements, or by pressing L. (The Advancements screen will be blank until you have accomplished at least one - the easiest may be creating your first crafting table.) Advancements are organized into tabs, and you can complete them in any order you wish. Tabs will open up through very basic in-game actions, like killing a mob or eating food.

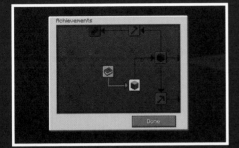

If you like playing with goals, use your achievement screen for new tasks.

You can track everything you've accomplished in your statistics screen, from how much iron you've mined to how many zombies you've killed.

There's also a way to "win" at Minecraft in a special final battle against the Ender Dragon in a realm called the End. It's difficult to get there, because to prepare you must learn how to use potions, kill Endermen, and survive the Nether to gather essential items. You can return to battle the Ender Dragon multiple times. Each time you defeat the dragon (up to twenty times), a new End gateway is created to take you to an Outer End Island with more places to explore.

## Making the Most out of Minecraft

### Don't Stress Out

You're going to die. Unless you are in Creative mode, something will get you at some point. Even in Peaceful mode, it might be a fall into a lava pool. But that is part of the game. Prepare for this as best you can by storing your goods in chests you can find later and, of course, remembering where your chests and home are.

### Switch It Up

If you need a break from the mobs for a bit, switch to Peaceful mode. To change the difficulty level in Survival, press Escape on your keyboard and change the options under Difficulty.

If you enabled cheats when you created your world, you can type commands in the chat window. Press t to open the window, and then type a slash and your command. /time set day changes the game to daytime.

### Use Cheats Wisely

Using cheats, or commands, can make survival game play feel less rewarding. But if you are playing in Creative mode and need to work free of mob attacks, you may want to also use commands. To use commands you must create your world with Cheats on. Then you can open up the chat window by pressing T. (The chat window only works for chatting if you are in multiplayer.) You type your command into the chat window, preceded by a slash. (You can also open up the chat window by typing the initial slash of the command.) So to change to Creative mode, type **/gamemode c**. To switch back to Survival mode, type **/gamemode s**. You can also change your difficulty level by typing **/difficulty 0** (for Peaceful) through **/difficulty 3** (Hard). Another popular cheat is to grant oneself experience, through **/xp X** (where X is the number of experience points). You can also teleport anywhere, if you know your coordinates, with **/tp X Y Z**. For a list of available commands, type **/help**.

**Worlds and Seeds**

If you just like to explore worlds, or if you're having a hard time finding structures like jungle temples, you can play in worlds other players have found. Each world is started with a "seed." When Minecraft creates a world, it generates a random number called a seed to spawn the world. You can see your world's seed by typing **/seed** in the chat window.

You can visit a world someone else found by entering the seed number for that world in your world's options screen.

You can also enter your own random number or sequence of characters in the More World Options screen, under Seed for the World Generator. Users share the seeds they have used online, at websites like minecraft-seeds.net. Find a world whose description you like at one of these sites, make sure the world was created using the same game version you are using, and type the seed for that world into your World Options screen. You can enter letters for a seed number, too. See what world is generated when you type in your own name! You can also change the basic type of world by clicking the World Type button:

- Superflat: A flat world with one grass layer above two dirt and one bedrock layer. You can customize the layers of a superflat world by clicking "Customize" or use some premade styles by clicking "Presets".

- Customized: Click this to turn on and off features like ravines, dungeon rarity, and more.

**Shortcuts to Manage Your Inventory**

Shortcut keys allow you to quickly move stuff between your inventory and other containers and slots. Your inventory consists of four armor slots, 27 storage slots, nine hotbar slots, and an off-hand slot.

- Press 1 through 9 to access the items in your hotbar.

- Press Shift and click to move a stack between your inventory and hotbar or between a container with an inventory and your hotbar/inventory.

- Shift-click armor to have it go straight into the right armor slots.

To access items in your hotbar quickly, type the number for that slot, from 1 to 9 (left to right).

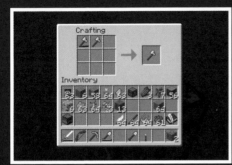

Repair your damaged tools by combining them with a new one. This gives them extra durability.

- Move items between the inventory and a specific slot in your hotbar by hovering over the item or blank slot in the inventory and pressing the number for that slot, from 0 to 9.
- Right-click to pick up half a stack.
- Double-click an item to pick up as many as a full stack (64) as available in your inventory.
- To move as many items of one kind as you can from your inventory to a chest, pick up any item, press Shift, and double-click the item you want to move.
- When you're crafting, you can right-click and drag over the slots to drop one item at a time from your stack into each slot. You can do this multiple times to keep adding an item to each slot.
- To craft as many items as possible from stacked craft slots, press Shift-click in the crafted item slot.

**Manage Your Tools**

Keep track of the damage your tools and weapons are taking, and repair them before they are broken. Craft one used tool with another tool of the same kind. With rare, fragile tools like Elytra, you will find it is more efficient to enchant them with Mending or Unbreaking before use.

## Modding Your Game

Minecraft was designed to allow other people to modify it. There are three main ways to customize your game. However, it is very easy to download an application or file that can damage your game or your computer. We recommend that if you do want to modify your game, you enlist the help of a parent or a friend who has already successfully done this. You need to make sure that any new files or applications you use are compatible with the exact version of the game you are playing; make backups of your game files before making any changes, and check for viruses!

- **Skins:** You can change the way your player character looks by uploading an image file, called a skin. You can find skins online or create your own using a skin editor. An easy way to change your skin is to download a skin that you like at a Minecraft skins website, like minecraftskins.com. Log in to your account at minecraft.net and go to your profile page. Click Browse to locate the new file on your computer and then Upload to change your skin.

A skin is a small image file that is used to show what your character looks like. Many games, including Minecraft, let you change your skin. This is a dragon found at minecraftskins.com.

- **Resource and texture packs**: These are sets of files that replace game resources like sounds, textures (image files) that make blocks look the way they do, and music. They don't change the basic way the game plays.

- **Mods:** Mods are programs you download that change something about the way the game operates. For example, one mod may add new biomes and plants; another might add new types of powerful tools and weapons.

- **Minecraft Marketplace:** If you play on a mobile, console, or Windows 10 edition of Minecraft, you can find tons of user-created maps, skins, and texture packs by clicking on the Store button. However, you do have to pay for them.

## Keep Learning!

Millions of people, adults and kids, play Minecraft. They are talking about Minecraft online, playing together in multiplayer games, and making videos and tutorials. Some of the best places to learn about Minecraft are from YouTube videos and at the Minecraft wiki at minecraft.gamepedia.com.

# CHAPTER 2

# NAVIGATING YOUR WORLD

Your Minecraft world is enormous. It has changing landscapes, called biomes, changing weather, and an endless numbers of caverns, lakes, seas, and lands. The downside is, there are no signs or guideposts. It is very easy to travel fast, chase a pig, flee from a creeper, get turned around, and get lost.

So a key strategy in Minecraft is to always know where you are, where home is, and how to get back. You probably have already learned to make a pillar beacon at your base. This can help to orient you if you are not too far away, but it won't help if you are very far away from home or if tall mountains are in the way. So when you build your pillar beacon, be sure it is higher than nearby mountains. Add more than one torch at the top to help blaze up the sky at night!

When you build a pillar beacon, make sure it is taller than surrounding mountains and is brightly lit.

Compasses and maps may seem like the answer, but a compass always points to your original spawn point. If you've reset your spawn point by sleeping in a bed somewhere else, the compass can't help. Maps work great, but to cover a large area you will need a set of large maps. To craft a large map or a zoomed out map, use a map in the crafting area center surrounded by eight papers. You can do this four times to create a map that is sixteen times as big as the original map size.

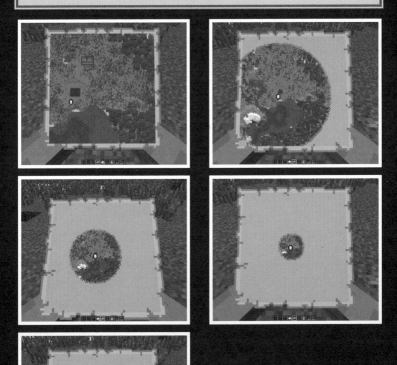

You can create four bigger sizes of a map from your first map.

A quick way to track your path as you go is to punch out the center sections of trees as you pass (if you are in a forest).

For a fast trail in a forest, punch out the centers of trees.

Or, if you are in a desert area, drop blocks of dirt (they'll stand out!). In a non-desert area, drop blocks of sand. You can use other blocks, just make sure they are easily noticeable in the landscape.

Leave blocks as breadcrumbs on your way.

If you're looking for or exploring interesting caves and ravines during your travels, mark them as you go. Use one type of marker to say, "Explore here!" and another to say, "Already explored." For a really important marker that you want to be able to spot easily, make a mini-tower with a torch.

You can use your own system and ideas for markers. This ravine has been marked with sand and red wool to show it's been explored.

## Using X and Z to Mark the Spot

Probably the best way to keep track of your home, and where you are at any time, is to use Minecraft's location coordinates, which you find by opening the Debug screen. To open the Debug screen, press and release F3 (or on some laptops, Fn+F3. Fn is the Function key). The Debug screen shows information about things like chunks (the sixteen-block sections of world that the Minecraft programming manages) and memory. The most important information for you is the X, Y, Z, and F numbers, which are near the bottom of the screen. With coordinates, the "center" of the world is at 0, 0, 0.

Listed toward the bottom of the debug screen are the X, Y, Z
coordinates and the direction you are facing in (F).

**X:** Shows where you are along an east-west line. Negative numbers show you are west of 0, 0.

**Z:** Shows where you are along a north-south line. Negative numbers show you are north of 0, 0.

**Y:** Shows the altitude or how high you are, from down in the mines (near 0) to mountains.

**F:** Shows you what direction you are facing—east, west, north, or south.

The important ones to record your location are the X and Z numbers. Keep a notebook (in the real world) to mark down the coordinates for home and other important places you find, like villages, temples, and abandoned mineshafts you want to explore. You could also keep a note on signs in your inventory, but these will be lost if you are killed.

When you get lost and you have your home base coordinates noted down somewhere, you can open up the Debug screen, look at your current X and Z position, and figure out what direction you need to go. It can be easiest to travel in one direction at a time, because the numbers on the Debug screen change very quickly, and it is hard to keep track of more than one number at a time. For example, if you need to go further east, concentrate on making sure you are facing east with the F number and then move in that direction. Keep looking at the screen to make sure that the X numbers are increasing (going further east) in your Debug screen. Of course, you may need to detour to avoid mountains or lakes!

## More Navigating Tips

- Clouds always travel west, so if you can't see the sun, you can tell the direction by the clouds.

- Bring a map underground—it will show if there is lava, sand, or water above you if you need to dig up.

- To mark your way, you can also remove the leaves from trees in your path, use dyed wool blocks, or use Jack o'Lanterns. You can use the face on the Jack o'Lantern to point the right direction!

When you place a Jack o'Lantern, its face is toward you. If you keep the faces all the same direction, this can help point you in the right direction.

## Traveling by Boat

In addition to traveling by foot and by horse, you can travel long distances by sea pretty fast, and if you have a river system, that is a good way to explore quickly. You can bring a passenger along to explore with you. If you hold a zoomed-out map, you can fill out a lot pretty quickly.

Exploring by boat.

- Use your movement keys - W, A, S, D, to control your movement. To prevent spinning around in your boat, just tap the A and D to turn left and right.

- You can even place your boat on land and drive it. You will go slowly, but it is a good way to transport villagers a short distance.

- Boats on ice are even faster!

- Your hunger bar stays at the same level when you travel by boat.

## Flying

Flying with your Elytra wings is one of the most fun ways to travel. Use firework rockets (paper and gunpowder) to speed up and counteract gravity pulling you back to the ground. You can also use these rockets to start flying right from the ground: Right click your rockets while you look up in the sky (so you don't set the rockets off against any blocks) then run and jump. At some point, a jump will register as the beginning of flight and the rockets will go off, allowing you to rise up into the air.

# CHAPTER 3
## EXPLORING

long with mining for rare ores and crafting cool objects, exploring your world is a major Minecraft activity. It's how you find rare plants, villagers to trade with, horses to tame, and temples to loot! One thing to know is what you can expect in all the different landscapes, or biomes, in Minecraft. You'll only find a jungle temple in the jungle, of course, but what can you find in the cold, snowy areas? Keep an eye out as you explore. You can use the Debug screen to find out exactly what biome you are in.

In the snowy biomes, the ones with spruce and oak trees (called "Taiga"), you can find wolves. Taiga is a name for coniferous northern forests; conifers have needle leaves. Cold biomes are rockier and have more trees than the snowy biomes. Wolves are more common in the cold Taiga biomes. In the medium and lush biomes you find plains, forests, swamplands, rivers, mushroom islands, beaches, and jungles. There are more ponds, rivers, and plants. Witch's huts are found in swamplands, and jungles are home to ocelots, cocoa beans, wild

To find what biome you are in, press F3 (or Fn + F3) to open the Debug screen and look for the entry "Biome". This is the Savanna biome.

melons, and jungle temples. Like the cold biomes, the dry or warm biomes have less animal and plant life. There are deserts with cactus, savannahs with acacia trees, and mesas with dry clay. You find villages in plains, deserts, and savannahs.

As you explore, look out for caves, ravines, villages, desert temples, jungle temples, igloos, and ocean monuments, as these are great places to find rare items that you cannot mine or craft. One of the most exciting structures to find is a woodland mansion. These are found only in roofed forests, and are so rare that you will need to trade with a village cartographer for a woodland explorer map. They're often thousands of blocks away from spawn. Occupied by "evil" villagers - the Vindicator and Evoker, you'll need some strong weaponry before you venture into these mazelike mansions.

## Exploring Caves

If you are exploring a cave system, it's especially easy to get turned around because it all kind of looks the same. A very simple way to mark your way is this: put torches on the right side of the cave wall, and only the right side, as you explore.

An easy way to keep track of your steps is by placing torches only on your right. Then to exit, make sure your placed torches are on your left. Mark any forks with a double torch showing the way back out.

When you retrace your steps back to the entrance, all you do is keep those torches to your left side. (You can do the opposite, too; just keep to the same tactic always.) When you use this tactic, be careful when you hit a fork. You need make sure to mark *which* fork leads toward the entrance. An easy way to do this is just leave two torches, one on top of the other.

When you reach a fork, use two torches to mark which way leads you back to the cave entrance.

If you are finished exploring a section, mark it done.

Use signs to leave notes for yourself ("Obsidian this way!" "Exit here!"). Use dashes and the greater than (>) sign to make arrows.

Use signs to show important finds and the exit

You can sometimes find a dungeon in a cave—these are cobblestone and mossy rooms that usually hold one (sometimes two) chests of loot. But watch out: there's also a mob spawner you will have to disarm!

Dungeons usually have chests with rare items—and a spawner!

## Abandoned Mineshafts

Abandoned mineshafts are created automatically with each new world. They are underground mazes of tunnels and shafts, partly broken up but lined and loaded with wood, rails, fencing, and cobwebs, ready to loot. You can also find chests that hold a few rare items like enchanted books and saddles, seeds, and often bread. There are torches already lit in these mineshafts, so there are fewer mobs, along with some treasure chests in minecarts. Of course, they do come with a downside—cave spider spawners. These are surrounded by thick layers of cobwebs. Cobwebs slow you down, but not the cave spiders! Cave spiders are smaller than regular spiders, so they can get through a 1×1 hole. Be warned!

You'll know you've found an abandoned mineshaft when you spot beams, posts, and tracks. Inside you'll find rails, ore, chests, and more to harvest.

Use shears to collect cobwebs or a sword to break them into string. Wall off the cave spider spawner and make sure the surrounding areas are lit up so that the spiders won't spawn outside of the walled off area. If you want to destroy the spawner, you can mine your way to just under (or over, or to the side of) the spawner's location and break it from a safe location. Kill cave spiders with a bow or sword, and take a pickaxe to destroy the spawner. If you are bitten by a spider, eat a golden apple or drink milk to heal. If part of a mineshaft is blocked by water or lava flow, see if there is any easy way to block that flow with cobblestone so you can keep exploring.

Despite the hazards, abandoned mineshafts are a treasure trove of loot. The easiest way to go looking for them is to look along the inside walls of ravines for the signs of a mineshaft below— wooden bridges crossing the ravine. Mineshafts also generate at higher levels in the Mesa biome, where you can easily spot entrances at ground level or in the side of hills.

### Getting Down a Ravine

There are several ways to get down a ravine. Drop blocks of sand or dirt at the edge, letting them drop all the way down. Once the stack is up to your level, jump on and dig down. Another way to get to the bottom of a ravine fast is to make a waterfall. A block or two from the edge of a ravine, pour some water so it flows into the ravine. Make sure that the wall you are pouring against goes straight down, and that there is a puddle of water at the bottom for you to land in. Step into the waterfall and let it carry you down. You can also swim back up a waterfall. Or, if you have a little time, just make steps down the side of the ravine. Depending on how the wall curves, you may need to dig in a little to turn a corner every once in a while.

One way to get down a steep cliff is to pour water over the side. Make sure the cliff edge is straight and the water ends in a puddle for you to land in.

## Desert Temples

Desert temples are another great source of loot, but you have to avoid or defuse the explosive TNT trap inside. When you enter through the main doors, there is an orange and blue stained clay block pattern in the floor. This hides a very deep chamber beneath, with a pressure plate connected to nine TNT blocks beneath the floor.

A desert temple.

At the edges of this hidden chamber are four chests holding rare and valuable loot such as diamonds, emeralds, enchanted books, and saddles.

Inside the temple is a floor that hides a chamber. In the chamber are four treasure chests, booby trapped to a pressure plate. If you touch the pressure plate, nine blocks of TNT will explode!

You need to get down to the bottom of this chamber without touching the pressure plate. Some people make a waterfall to swim down, but this gets you pretty close to the pressure plate. A safer way is to dig a staircase down the sides of the chamber; you can even dig straight down the wall. Then you can break the pressure plate, loot the chests, and collect the TNT and the chests.

## Ocean Monuments

You'll find ocean monuments only in deep ocean. They are dark, large, mazelike structures made from rare blocks like prismarine, dark prismarine, and ocean lanterns. They hold a hidden treasure in their central room: 8 gold blocks wrapped in dark prismarine. You will also find the fierce ocean mobs—the guardian

d the two mightier elder guardians—that protect the monu-
ent from you! To fight these you will definitely need potions,
chantments, and a very sharp sword. If an ocean monument
near land, you could try tunneling to it. Find the coordinates
the center of the monument as you boat over. Then tunnel
m land to the bottom center of the monument. It is easier to
ht guardians inside the monument, because it is harder for
em to dart away.

op of an ocean monument is close to the surface, so watch out for rectangula
es in the deep ocean biome.

## le Temples

e desert temples, jungle temples have both loot and booby
ps. The jungle temple has two chests. On one side of the tem-
is a lever puzzle you must solve to open up the hole to one
est. There are three levers, and you must play with these to
e what order of up and down will reveal the chest.

Like desert temples, jungle temples have both loot and booby traps. The jungle temple has two chests. On one side of the temple is a lever puzzle you must solve to open up the hole to one chest. There are three levers, and you must play with these to see what order of up and down will reveal the chest.

Go down the main stairs in a jungle temple to find the puzzle and the booby traps. On one side of the stairs is a puzzle of three levers.

On the other side of the temple, there is a corridor that is booby trapped with trip wires. If you set off the trip wires, this will trigger a dispenser that will fire arrows right at you! Go in the temple front doors—there will be a level above and below you. Below you on one side of the stairs are the three levers; on the other side is the booby-trapped hallway.

The trip wire is very hard to see. It is a little line that crosses across the floor of the hall. It's easier to spot the trip wire hooks on the sides of the corridor. Use a pickaxe to break up the trip wire hooks and disarm the trip wire. You can also cut the trip wire with shears. At the end of the corridor is the dispenser in the wall, covered in vines, which you can right click to loot the arrows. Be careful—a little further along is another trip wire in front of another dispenser, guarding a chest. Disarm the trip wire in the same way!

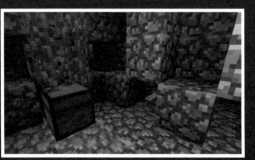

Once you get past the first set of trip wires in the jungle temple, there is another set. The trip wire hook is to the right, and the arrow dispenser is hidden in vines above the chest.

For the lever puzzle, the combination depends on whether the levers are to the right or the left of the stairs back up. On the right of the stairs, click the furthest right lever, the furthest left lever, then the middle. Then, flick the middle one up, then the left, then the right. For levers that are to the left of the stairs, flip down the left, right, then middle, and flip up the middle, right, and left. Go up the stairs. A hole has opened in the floor. Dig down to get to that area to find the second chest! Along with the chest treasure, collect all the special blocks used in making the traps and levers work: trip wire, dispensers, pistons, redstone, and redstone repeater.

## More Exploring Tips

- Always carry a full stack of torches so you can light passageways and caves as you go to prevent mobs from spawning.

- Ladders are a great way to travel up and down fast. You can use the sneak key (Shift key) to pause while you're on a ladder.

- At the edge of a cliff or ravine, use the sneak key. This lets you move very slowly a little distance over the edge so you can peer below. You can also use this to help you build a bridge right in front of you, over lava pools, in deep holes, and across ravines.

# CHAPTER 4

# MINING

If you're playing Minecraft, then you've probably logged quite a few hours hacking into the ground and caves. You've amassed a good loot of coal, iron, and even diamonds and redstone. But getting all this great loot out of the ground takes some time, especially if you haven't found enough diamonds for making the strongest pickaxe. Over the years, miners of the world have debated what the best tactics are for spending the least amount of time and getting the most amount of stuff. Here are some of the best tactics to take you to the top of the leaderboard in mining.

## Plan Your Trip!

If you're going mining, take enough essentials to last. At the very least you'll want a good stack of torches, a crafting table, several pickaxes and shovels, and plenty of food. There's not much food underground, or much wood (unless you run into an abandoned mineshaft!), so bring a stack of logs and plenty of munchies.

## The Safest Mining

Want to avoid the skeletons and cave spiders but don't want to change to Peaceful mode? Since mobs spawn in the dark, control the dark. Start mining from scratch in your own protected home, and make sure you are well lit all the way down. If you come across the opening to a dark cave, block it off. Mark the opening somehow, in case you want to explore later. You could even put a door there!

To mine monster-free, mine from home and keep well lit all the way!

## Choose Your Tools

Remember to dig with the right tools, using the most durable tool you have. Use the pickaxe for ore and cobblestone and use a shovel for dirt, gravel, and sand. Keep your tools in the same spot on your hotbar, so that you can always type a 1, for example, to get your pickaxe. This makes switching between tools easy and fast.

If you keep the
same slots in y
type the numb
you can be ver
between tools

## Level 11

All the different types of ore—from charcoal to dia
found between different levels in the ground. The
el in the Overworld, level 0, is bedrock. Bedrock is
can't get through it, you can't mine it, and it's indest
what separates the Overworld from the Nether.

The next block up from bedrock is level 1, then level 2, and so forth. You can find diamond between levels 1 and 15, emerald between 4 and 31, and coal on most levels. There's been a lot of research into what ore is found in what concentrations at what levels. Long story short, for the greatest chances of finding all the rarer ores, as well as common ores, dig down to level 11. To see what level you are at, open up your Debug screen by pressing F3. In your x, y, and z coordinates, the y coordinate will show you what level you are at. (It will actually show you what level your feet are at, and what approximate level your eyes are at!)

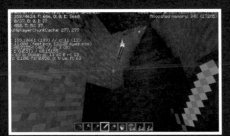

On average, you'll find the most ores of all types at level 11.
To check your level, open your debug screen and look at the Y coordinate.

Another way to get to bedrock is to just dig down to bedrock and count up the blocks from there. Now, some people swear by mining at level 10, and others by level 12. So you are probably doing fine at any of these levels.

## Efficient Exits

Conserve energy on your mining returns. Instead of jumping up

Jumping up mine steps can sap your energy, so consider placing stairs on top of those blocks. You can travel stairs with no extra energy loss.

Or, instead of digging steps down, create a ladder shaft. (Remember not to dig straight down for a ladder shaft. Dig two blocks wide down, moving from block 1 to block 2 as you dig the next block down, placing the ladder pieces along one side.)

To dig a ladder shaft straight down, dig one block in front of you, hop into that, and dig the block you were just standing on. Repeat, placing ladder pieces along one side.

## Space-Efficient Entries

If you don't want to travel far from your starting point at ground level, or you just want to use space more efficiently, create a spiral staircase. The tightest spiral staircase takes up a 2 × 2 block area. To make it, dig one block in front of you. Step into that hole, turn right, and dig the block in front of you and one block down. Step into that hole, turn right, and dig out the next step. Keep doing that until you get down as far as you want to go. You can make wider spiral staircases, too!

Spiral staircases and ladder shafts save space so you aren't traveling too far in one direction from where you start the descent.

## Branch Mining

When you really just want to get as much stuff as possible, one of the most efficient ways to get the most ore out of a big area is through branch mining. You start off with a central room or hall and then mine corridors off from that, spacing the corridors four blocks apart (with three blocks between each corridor). If you want to make sure you see every single possible piece of ore, keep two blocks between the corridors. But since most veins of ores are a couple blocks long or more, you can save time and not lose much by placing your shafts four blocks apart.

A branch mine has shafts dug out every three or four blocks.

## Cave Mining

If you're fine with battling mobs as you go, or you mine in Peaceful mode, use your world's caves and ravines as your mines. With cave mining, also called spelunking, there's a lot less digging, so it's fast! Follow the cave branches to the lowest they go, then dig with a pickaxe deeper down to level 11 and start a branch mine from there. One way to minimize the mobs is to fully explore and light it with torches first.

## TNT

You can find blocks of TNT in desert temples (in traps!), or you can create it from sand (red or yellow) and gunpowder. A TNT blast will create a hole in a mountain or the ground. While it will blow out some whole blocks, most blocks are destroyed. It's not a great tactic for collecting ore, but it is a fun option for making a crater! Place your TNT, "prime it" (meaning light it) by right-clicking with your flint and steel, and step away fast. TNT blocks flash several times before they detonate, giving you time to escape. If you don't mind losing ore on your way down, you can blast your way down to lower levels.

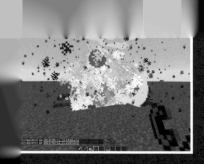

If for some reason you need to blow a big hole in something, use TNT. While a TNT blast does scatter some blocks, it destroys most of them, so it isn't a great option for getting ore.

## Build a Base

Once you've reached level 11, or wherever you want to start mining from, make a base camp. If you are planning to spend some time down there, you'll want a protected area with a bed and a chest or two to store your findings. Also place a furnace or two so you can smelt your ores as you mine, as well as a crafting table to make more shovels and pickaxes.

Build a base camp when you are down in your mine.

Enchant your diamond pickaxe, axe, and shovel! The Efficiency enchantment increases your mining speed. Silk Touch lets you collect some blocks that you can't get otherwise, like emerald ore (which you'd normally collect as a single emerald, rather than a block). Unbreaking makes your tools more durable, and Fortune gives you a chance of collecting more ore per block.

## Obsidian

Obsidian is the toughest block in Minecraft except for bedrock (which you can't mine) and is a great building material against creepers. It is also required for building Nether portals and enchantment tables. Although it is pretty rare, you can find it in low levels, often by lava. Obsidian is created when running water hits a lava source, and there is plenty of lava at low levels when you mine. You can re-create this yourself, or be very careful when mining it, as there is a good chance that lava is nearby, even under one layer of obsidian. If you see the source of flowing water, there is a chance that digging will release the flow, pushing you around. One tactic is to block the flowing water so you have no surprises when you are digging out the obsidian.

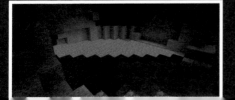

Obsidian, the toughest block except for bedrock, is formed when lava meets running water.

## More Tips on Mining

- Have blocks of stone or dirt at the ready in case you need to block a lava or water flow.

- To get rid of a column of gravel at once, destroy the bottom block and quickly place a torch in its place. The torch will destroy the gravel blocks falling down from above.

- Place torches no more than twelve blocks apart to keep the light level high enough to prevent mobs spawning. Use more torches if there are corners in the walls blocking light.

- To gather all the rails in an abandoned mineshaft, just pour a bucket of water into one end—the flowing water will pull up all the rails, ready to pop into your inventory.

# CHAPTER 5

# FIGHTING

**U**nless you've been playing in Creative mode or at Peaceful difficulty, you have been attacked by zombies, spiders, and skeletons and have lived to see the day. Now you want to improve your skills and up your chances of coming out on the winning side. If you want to make it through the Nether to gather rare items and travel to the End to defeat the dragon, you'll need to hone your tactics.

## Practice, Practice, Practice!

One way to improve your skills is to create a world that's only for practicing fighting. Don't worry about how many times you are killed. Create the world with cheats turned on and start in Creative mode. Use your creative mode inventory to place chests of armor, weapons, chests, food, and everything else you need, then switch back to Survival. Set your difficulty level at whatever you are comfortable with and wait for the mobs with your sword ready. If you are experienced with downloading maps or have some help with this, you can also download maps that have been created by other users, just for practicing. (See Chapter 16: The End and Beyond on page 139 to find out more about maps.) They may have contraptions that spawn zombies or a target practice range. You can also easily create your own valley and build targets to shoot. For moving targets, populate your shooting range with sheep using Creative mode sheep spawners. Add a mountain ledge to shoot from and a chest or more of arrows, and practice your bow and arrow skills!

If you need bow and arrow practice, make your own shooting range! Create a target from dyed wool and fill the range with passive mobs to shoot at.

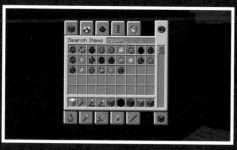

In Creative mode, your inventory includes spawn eggs for each type of mob. Place an egg on the ground to spawn the mob.

## ttack!

In older versions, a fast attack was the best attack. With the Combat Update, rapid-fire attacks deliver less damage than well-timed hits. Check the attack indicator in your toolbar to time your attacks when your weapon is fully charged. You'll deliver the most damage with a charged weapon. When you can, use your shield in the off-hand slot to block blows and arrows as your weapon strength recharges.

Use your shield to block and incoming attack while your weapon recharges to full power.

This can decrease the attack damage done to you by two-thirds, and will completely block damage from projectiles like arrows and snowballs. (When you block with a shield, you move at a slow speed.) As you practice flailing or block-hitting, quickly alternate between attack (left-click) and block (right-click). If you are too close to an exploding creeper, use a shield to block yourself from taking any damage. When you deliver damage to a mob, it turns red. While it is red, you can't deliver any more damage, so wait a moment or fight a different mob. If you can, lead them to a better fighting area. Most mobs switch to a pursuit mode if they are within sixteen blocks of you and can directly see you.

**Critical Hits**
To make the most of your attack, jump and deliver your blow as you fall. This gives a critical hit that delivers up to 50 percent more damage, and this can make a huge difference. You can tell you've delivered a critical hit when stars float over your opponent. You can also deliver a critical hit when jumping off a block. A critical hit with an arrow occurs if your arrow is fully pulled back before you shoot. You can tell your arrow is fully charged when your bow shakes slightly.

To cause the most damage, jump and then swing on your way down for a critical hit. If you give one, you'll see little stars over your victim.

### Knockbacks

If you are sprinting before the blow, you knock back the enemy. Knocking back a creeper may give you more time to escape. However, knocking back a skeleton gives it a chance to re-arm, so don't use this tactic with them. You can knock back entities with chicken eggs or snowballs.

## Minecraft Enemies

### Cave Spiders

Cave spiders only spawn from spawners in abandoned mineshafts. (Spawners are cage-like boxes that spawn a hostile mob every few seconds if you are near them.) They are faster than regular spiders and poisonous. Often the best solution is to block off the spawner area as fast as you can. Light up the area around the spawner to stop if from spawning spiders outside of the blocked off area. If you move fast enough, and you don't want to save the spawner for a mob farm, just break the spawner itself.

You'll probably first hear the skritching sounds of the cave spiders before you see their lair of thick cobwebs. Use blocks to prevent them getting near you!

### Creepers

If a creeper is suddenly next to you, run away. You have about 1.5 seconds, once it starts detonating, to get about five blocks away. If you do, the creeper will halt the process. It will still be after you, though! Try to get far away from them and then attack them with a bow. If you need to fight them close up, hit them with your sword and then back away quickly.

### Enderman

Making sure your crosshairs don't move above the Enderman's legs (so as not to provoke it), attack its feet. Move to or create a shelter that is only two blocks high—so that an Endermen can't enter. Provoke the enderman by looking at it (if you aren't already) and then strike at its legs.

### Endermites

Endermites are small like silverfish. They are weak (8 hearts) so just slash at them as quickly as you can—your attack indicator doesn't need to be completely full.

### Evokers

Try to keep a good distance from them (and away from their Fang attacks) and shoot them with a bow. Try to kill them before they spawn the vexes.

### Guardians and Elder Guardians

You'll need a sharp sword and potions. Corner them quickly inside the monument so they can't escape.

### Silverfish

These small, bug-like mobs hide in silverfish blocks that look like stone or granite in Extreme Hill biomes, in igloos, and in stronghold dungeons. If you break one of these blocks, the silverfish, and sometimes surrounding silverfish, will come out to attack you as a group. To kill them, use a steel and flint to set them on fire, or drop a bucket of lava on them (stand on a block to do this!). You can also drop gravel on them. If you attack them indirectly like this without a sword, it stops them from alerting their allies.

### Shulker

Time your arrows to hit the shulker's tender body as it opens its hard shell up.

### Skeletons

Skeletons are very difficult to fight, unless you have a shield, and then they are easy. Sneak up to them with your shield out to block their arrows. Then time your blows right after they shoot each arrow. Watch out for the skeleton variant Strays in the frozen biomes. Strays have arrows that will affect you with Slowness.

### Slime

Attack them from above. Kill the big ones first, then move to the smaller ones.

### Spiders

Because of their jumping abilities, hit them and walk backward.

### Spider Jockeys

Kill the skeleton first and then the spider.

### Vexes

Spawned by Evokers, you'll want to kill them before their Evoker if the Evoker is far away. Strike at them as they head towards you.

### Vindicators

Vindicators deal a lot of damage and will run fast at you, so be prepared with a shield and your strongest sword.

### Witches

Because they can throw potions at you, kill witches with a bow. Or move very fast to attack the witch before it has time to drink Fire Resistant and Instant Health potions to protect itself.

Use your bow to kill witches, or attack them before they drink their potion and splash you with one.

### Zombies

Hitting a zombie can draw others to the fight, so first see if you can lead them outside to burn in the sun. Husks, a zombie variant you will find in deserts, can give you the hunger effect, and don't burn in the sun!

### Zombie XP farm

Mob experience farms are ways to get lots of experience points (XP). These farms create large numbers of mobs in an enclosed space as well as a safe place for you to kill them. In a simple zombie XP farm, first find a zombie mob spawner in a dungeon and disarm it. Build a 8 x 8 chamber around the spawner, with a 2×1 shaft along one of the longest walls, in the center. The shaft should be less than twenty-three blocks deep. (A twenty-two-block fall will leave creepers, zombies, and skeletons with a half heart of life left, so they'll be fast to kill and provide experience orbs.) You can use water flows to push the zombies to the pit. When you pour water, the water flows for eight blocks and then stops. Use a bucket to pour water at the opposite corners from the shaft. The two water flows should stop at the edge of the shaft, without going into the shaft. (If they don't, you may need to make the room a block or two bigger.)

Enclose the zombie spawner so that water placed at one side will push zombies through a shaft at the other end.

Next, on the outside of the chamber, and on the outside of the zombie shaft, create another ladder shaft for you that is one block deeper. Dig a 1×1 hole between you and the zombie shaft so you can attack the zombies' feet with a sword. You will need to plan your build so that you can re-arm the spawner, barricade the room, then get down your ladder shaft to your killing cubicle! There are hundreds of types of mob spawners and tutorials online with different ways to kill mobs of mobs. For a different type of mob farming that gets you more loot without moving a muscle, see the mob farm instructions in chapter 8.

Build your separate access to the zombie drop so that there is a one-block-high hole you can attack them through.

## More Mob Fighting Tips

- For extra defense, tame wolves and ocelots. Tamed wolves will attack your enemies in battle and a tamed ocelot will scare creepers away.

- A creeper that is hit with lightning becomes "charged" with a bluish light and then can deliver even more explosive force—more than a TNT block. A skeleton, zombie, or creeper that is killed by the explosion of a charged creeper will drop its head.

- Running from a creeper? By sprinting and jumping at the same time, you'll go faster than if you are just sprinting.

- You can wear a pumpkin on your head and look at an Enderman without provoking it.

- To get twice as close to creepers, skeletons, or zombies without being seen as a threat, wear a head that matches the mob you want to approach.

# CHAPTER 6
## ANIMALS

nimals are essential to surviving and thriving in your Minecraft world. You use them to help and protect you, give you food, and keep you company! Animals are a type of mob in Minecraft called a passive mob, because they don't attack you. By now you've probably tamed and bred sheep, chicken, goats, and pigs, but there is much more fun to have with them.

Where do you find the animals? Sheep, horses, and cows like open fields with grass. Go to a jungle to find an ocelot, and go to forests and plains for pigs. To lure animals back to your farm, use the same items as you would to breed them. With the lured item in your hand, get close to the animal. When you see the animal turn to look at you and take a few steps toward you, it is interested! Make your way slowly back home with the lure item in your hand. Sometimes animals lose interest, so keep an eye out for animals that have stopped following you. You will need to re-interest them! You can also use a lead to pull an animal along, or push one into a boat that you can sail towards home.

### Mooshroom

A mooshroom is one of the strangest and rarest animals! It looks like a cow painted as a red mushroom, with red mushrooms growing on its back. The only place you can find them is on a rare Mushroom Island biome. You can milk a mooshroom with an empty bowl for mushroom stew! And if you shear the mushrooms off its back, it will turn back into a cow.

The mooshroom is a hybrid cow/mushroom. If you shave its mushrooms, it turns back into a cow.

The mushroom biome also grows giant mushrooms on a special dirt-like block called mycelium. You can break a giant mushroom for a mushroom harvest.

The Mushroom Island biome is rare, and it's the only place you can find the mooshroom creature!

## Wolf Pets

Unlike farm animals and ocelots, wolves are actually a neutral mob, like Endermen. If you attack a wolf, you will be attacked back, likely by its whole pack. Once you tame a wolf, though, it is a protective friend. It will follow you wherever you go and attack anything that attacks you. If your wolf is far from you and you are attacked, it will teleport to you. Unlike farm animals, wolves need to be fed. You can tell how healthy a wolf is by its tail. If it's sticking straight out, it's doing great. Its tail starts to angle down as it loses health, but a meal of meat (cooked is best) will help restore it. Tamed and wild wolves attack skeletons automatically, and skeletons will run from them!

You can tell a wol is healthy if its tail is straight out If your wolf's tail droops, it is time to feed it.

## Tame an Ocelot

Creepers are scared of ocelots! Tame an ocelot so it will help stop creepers getting close to your home. An ocelot can only be tamed if it is in begging mode, which means it is slowly walking toward you and looking at you. But you can't make any sudden moves or turns or it will stop begging and go away. Taming an ocelot is a tricky business.

Keep very still as you try to tame an ocelot. It may flee with sudden movements.

## Taming and Riding Horses

Riding a horse is the fastest way to travel on ground in Survival mode. Horses can jump up to four blocks high, ride over one-block holes in the ground, and jump over larger holes. To keep a horse, you will need to find a wild one, tame it, and outfit it with a saddle. To tame a horse, you must mount it by right-clicking on it with your hand. The horse will probably throw you off, so keep doing this until hearts float above its head and it lets you stay on. It may take five or more tries.

To dismount the horse, use the sneak key. Now the horse is tamed, but it won't follow you around like a tamed wolf or ocelot. You will need to either ride it or keep a lead on it and tie the lead to a fence post. You craft a lead with string and slimeball.

In order to ride the horse, place a saddle on it by right-clicking on the saddle. (To get a rare Minecraft saddle, you will have to trade with a villager or find one in a chest.) If you are on the horse already, open your inventory. Your inventory contains a horse inventory slot now, and you can place the saddle into these slots. You can also outfit your horse with armor. Like saddles, horse armor can only be found in chests.

The horse inventory appears above your horse. To saddle a horse, drag a saddle to it.

You can ride a horse in the same way you move about, with the keyboard controls and mouse. You will also see, above your hotbar, the horse's jump bar in place of your experience bar. Your health bar is replaced with the horse's health bar.

When you ride a horse, your display shows the horse's health and a jump bar in place of your health and experience bars.

## More Horse Tips

- To make your horse jump, hold down the jump key (space bar) and release when you are ready. Some horses can jump up four or more blocks high.

- You can fight on horses, just like on foot, as well as mine and collect dropped items.

- Breed horses with golden apples or golden carrots. Golden apples are rare items you can find sometimes in dungeon chests. You craft a golden carrot from eight golden nuggets and a regular carrot.

- Feed foals (young horses) so they grow faster. To restore the health of damaged horses, feed them with wheat, sugar, apples, bread, hay bales, and golden carrots and apples. Hay bales are made from nine blocks of wheat. (If you place a hay bale into your crafting table, it will give nine blocks of wheat. This makes it a great way to travel with lots of wheat!)

- Not all horses are the same—some are faster and can jump higher than others.

- Horses don't like water, and you will be dismounted if you ride in water deeper than two blocks. You may need to use a lead to get them through water.

- You can also leash wild horses.

## About Skeleton Trap Horses

If you come within ten blocks of certain horses, there is a small chance you will trigger a skeleton trap. The horse will be struck by lightning and transform into a skeleton horse and rider. Three other skeleton pairs will appear nearby. They spawn with enchanted helmets and bows and fight like skeletons, strafing ahead to attack and backing up when approached. If they spawn in the Nether, there's a good chance the rider will be a wither skeleton.

Donkeys are smaller than horses, have a grayish-brown coat, and have tall ears. Like horses, though, they can be fed and bred the same way. You can place a chest on them and fill the chest up with supplies! You create mules only by breeding a horse with a donkey. Mules look like donkeys but have a darker coat. They can also be equipped with a chest.

**Right-click a tamed donkey or mule with a chest. The donkey's inventory will hold fifteen items.**

## Animal Farms

When you design your animal enclosures, be sure to add in a double gate system. This adds an additional exterior pen as a fenced and gated walkway. That way, when an animal escapes its pen (and they all do at some point), it will still be fenced in within the general enclosure, and you will have a much easier time getting them back in their pen. If you are breeding chickens, remember they can jump over a single-block high fence, so you'll need to make their fences higher or dig a level down in their pen.

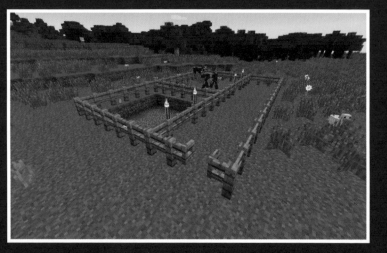

For animal pens, use a double gated system. If an animal escapes from its pen, there is a second gated pen to prevent it running away.

## More Animal Tips

- Squids can't be bred, but you can kill them for sacs of black ink, which you can use as a dye.

- Bats seem to be pretty useless—they don't drop anything or provide food. But they do make a squeaking noise, and if you are digging a mine, hearing that squeak means a cave is nearby.

- Don't kill all the animals in a group. Friendly mobs spawn extremely rarely so you will have lost a potential source of animals. At the very least, leave a couple to breed, or bring two back for your own breeding farm.

- If you kill a sheep, it drops wool (and meat). But you'll get more wool if you use your shears.

- You can throw a chicken's egg, and sometimes they'll hatch into a chicken on the spot! There's even a rare chance for quadruplets.

- Breed rabbits for their great drops: rabbit meat (for stew), feet (for potions of leaping), and rabbit hide (4 of these will make 1 regular leather.) You can breed rabbits with dandelions and golden carrots as well as carrots.

- If you name a rabbit Toast with a nametag, the rabbit will take on a custom black and white rabbit skin. The skin is a memorial for a pet rabbit that belonged to a friend of one of the game developers.

- You can speed up how fast baby animals turn into adults by feeding them their favorite food (the same used for breeding). Each time you feed it, you will take off about 10 percent of the growth time left.

- Tame a llama by right-clicking it to ride, multiple times, until you see hearts. Breed llamas with hay bales. Llamas are hostile to untamed wolves, so they make good protectors for your sheep.

- Polar bears that have young will attack you if you get too close—so steer clear!

- Parrots will imitate the sounds of nearby mobs—but not consistently enough to make them good alerts for you.

# CHAPTER 7
## VILLAGES AND VILLAGERS

**L**ike pyramids and abandoned mineshafts, villages and villagers are a great source for rare items in Minecraft. You can trade for items with villagers, find carrots and potatoes in their farms and books in their libraries, and loot the occasional chest! Villages can be found in the desert, plains, taiga, and savanna biomes, although they are pretty rare. Villages in the plains and savanna are built mostly with wood and cobblestone, while villages in the desert are made from sandstone, and taiga villages use spruce wood and logs.

A village in the desert and savanna will have the same types of buildings, just constructed with "local" materials.

In addition to huts, houses, and farms, villages have several specialized buildings. You can find butcher shops, libraries, smithies, and churches. Butcher shops have tables and stone slab counters, libraries have bookshelves, smithies have furnaces and a chest, and churches have an altar.

A butcher shop, library, smithy, and church.

## Help the Village!

Villages have a hard time surviving because they attract zombies who turn the inhabitants into zombie villagers. If you are playing in Hard difficulty, zombies can even break down their wooden doors. Villagers don't breed quickly, and they can accidentally die by stepping into lava or a cactus. Overall, that means a village can have trouble keeping its numbers up.

To cure a zombie villager, isolate it, splash it with a Potion of Weakness, and feed it a golden apple. The villager will shake for a few minutes before it recovers.

**How to Help Save a Village**

- Sleep inside it as soon as dusk falls. When you sleep, the game changes the time of day to dawn. This means that night is "skipped," along with the darkness that allows mobs to spawn. This minimizes zombies from spawning. In the morning, kill off the zombies.

- Fence the village in. You can also lock villagers in their homes until the fencing is done, to keep them safe.

- Remove stairs in front of doors, replace broken doors, and make sure doors are hung properly from the outside. (Do not add a door to the smithy, though. Because of the way the building is constructed, this confuses the villagers and prompts them to gather outside.)

- Light the outside of the village up to prevent mob spawning.

- Fix hazards, such as nearby cactus, pools of lava, and mob-spawning caves.

- If you can, cure zombie villagers by splashing them with a Potion of Weakness and feeding them a golden apple. It takes a few minutes for a zombie villager to heal, so make sure the zombie villager is isolated (and protected from sunlight) and can't hurt other villagers or you in the meantime. When a zombie villager is healed, it will return to its former profession.

- You can also protect your villagers with Iron Golems, and you can make new houses to increase your village and give them a better chance of survival.

### Iron Golems

Iron Golems only spawn naturally if a village has ten villagers and twenty-one houses. If the village doesn't have an Iron Golem, make one. You can create an Iron Golem with a pumpkin or Jack o'Lantern head and four blocks of iron in a T, placed on the ground (not in a crafting table). Iron Golems protect villagers only, and if they aren't in a village, they can wander away. You can keep Iron Golems in a fenced area or leash it to follow you.

Place the pumpkin or lantern last when you make an Iron Golem.

### Trading

The types of trading offers that a villager makes to you depend on their job. (Green-robed villagers are the only ones who don't trade.) In general, you buy with emeralds or sell goods to receive emeralds. The first time you trade with a villager, there will be just one offer. They will make new offers once you've traded for the last item in their list and closed the inventory window. If they have a new offer for you, you'll see green and purple particles over their head.

When a villager has a new offer, you will see green and purple particles over him.

There are hundreds of trading offers. Also, different villagers of the same type can offer better or worse deals. One weapon smith might offer a great deal of 12 emeralds for a diamond pick, and another weapon smith's offer might be more expensive. A great tactic is to find several villagers that have good deals giving you emeralds for something you can get easily and for free, and keep them safe and separated so you can find them again. For example, you may find a farmer that will give you 1 emerald for 7 melons. Or a librarian who will give you an emerald for 21 paper. You can then trade with villagers librarians to get masses of emeralds. When the villager's trade expires, you will need to buy something else for a while to get them to re-offer the deal you want. Once you have your emeralds in hand, you then want to find several villagers with the best deals on stuff that is difficult to get in the game. A cleric may have a good deal on Bottles o' Enchanting (3 emeralds is great!), and a tool smith may have a great deal on diamond picks. Here are the villager types and what they trade in:

**Armorer:** Buys coal, iron, and diamonds; sells axes and swords.
**Butcher:** Buys raw pork, raw chicken, and coal; sells cooked pork and chicken.
**Cartographer:** Like the librarian, but sells maps, ocean explorer maps (to find guardian temples), and woodland explorer maps (to find woodland mansions).
**Cleric:** Buys zombie flesh and gold; sells lapis, redstone, glowstone, Ender pearls, Bottles o' Enchanting, and redstone.
**Farmer:** Buys farm produce; sells bread, pastries, and apples.
**Fisherman:** Buys fish, coal, and string; sells fishing rods.
**Fletcher:** Buys string and gravel; sells bows and arrows.
**Leatherworker:** Buys leather; sells leather armor and saddles.
**Librarian:** Buys paper and books; sells enchanted books, compasses, bookshelves, glass, and nametags.
**Shepherd:** Buys wool; sells wool and shears.
**Tool Smith:** Buys coal, iron, and diamonds; sells shovels and picks.
**Weapon Smith:** Buys coal, iron, and diamonds; sells axes and swords.

Eleven types of trading villagers have five costumes. A cleric is in purple, and armorers, tool smiths, and weapon smiths are in black. Librarians and cartographers wear white, and butchers and leatherworkers have a white apron. Farmers, fishermen, fletchers, and shepherds all wear brown.

### Increase the Population

Add new houses to the village. In order for the Minecraft program to recognize you have made a new house, it must first see a new door. To make sure that the door counts as a house, the program checks to see if there is a roof on one side of the door. As long as you follow these guidelines, you can make your village houses however you like. Because of the way the program works, you can build a door with just one block of roof. Here is what the program looks for: After you've built a door, it looks at the five spaces directly in front of and in back of the door to check for roof blocks. A roof block is any block preventing sunlight from hitting the ground. There must be more roof blocks on one side of the door than the other. (This means you can make a house from just a block of dirt and a door, if you are low on resources.) Finally, to count as a house, the door must be near a villager. For every three-and-a-half new doors, a new villager will be created, so to get two villagers, make seven doors. For the villagers to make children, there must be at least two villagers.

To add the simplest village house, you just need a door and one roof block behind it.

**Be Nice!**
You have a popularity score with each village. It starts at 0, increases to a high of 10, and can decrease to -30. Trading with a villager for the last offer slot in their inventory adds one point. You get points taken off for attacking a villager (-1), killing a villager (-2), killing a village child (-3), and killing the village's Iron Golem (-5). If you have a score of -15, the village's Iron Golem will attack you.

## More Village Tips

- Zombie sieges happen more often in large villages with forty or more villagers.

- Villages spawn more frequently in the superflat terrain and in worlds created with the Large Biomes option.

- Village wells are an easy place for players and villagers to fall in, and they are too deep to jump out of. Put blocks at the bottom of the well so they aren't a death trap.

Put blocks at the bottom of a well so they can get out!

# CHAPTER 8

## BUILDING

**Y**our home in Minecraft can be anything from a temporary shelter while you explore the world or a massive fortress that keeps you safe from the mobs. There's no right way to build your home—it all depends on how you play your game and what you want.

There are many great places to build a home, too. Build on a cliff or mountain, or build a tower if you want a great lookout. If you build on flat land, you'll have an easier time expanding with farms and contraptions. If you need shelter in a hurry, mine into the side of a mountain. You can even set your home up in a cave, walling off areas as you need. You can build a treehouse, or even build your home under water. If you don't want to build too much but want a pretty nice home, think about taking over a village home or even a temple. (For a village home, be prepared to battle and defend against extra zombies looking for villager snacks.)

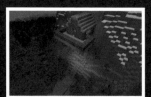

You have endless choices for building your Minecraft base. Make the swamps your home, or disguise your home as a tree!

In any location you choose, there are ways to make sure the home you build is safe from creeper explosions and unexpected spider attacks. One thing to keep in mind is whether your defensive building techniques are putting you in danger in addition to the mobs. You don't want to fall into your own cactus and lava pits! Possibly the safest home is one built underground and well lit, where no mobs can spawn.

A fairly simple way to protect your homestead is to guard it with a full perimeter wall three blocks high. The wall should have an overhang (using slabs) to prevent spiders from jumping over it, or a top layer of glass (which spiders can't climb), and should also be well lit. Make sure the area outside your defending wall is clear, and that there are no trees or high ground that a mob can jump on to get over the wall.

A three-block-high defensive perimeter wall with a lip to stop spiders from crawling over.

For extra flair, make a way to help kill stray mobs coming up to your house. On the outside of the wall, dig a series of two-block-deep pits for mobs to fall into. On the inside of the wall, dig yourself a tunnel or a short ladder shaft to access your pits. You should be one level deeper than the mob pit. Make a one block hole between your side and the foot of the pit. This is often called a "murder hole." It allows you to attack the feet of the trapped mobs and gather the loot they drop.

Dig two-block-deep pits outside your defensive wall to trap mobs. On the inside of the wall, make a murder hole from where you can kill them.

**More Tips on Defensive Building**

- Spiders can't climb up glass or iron bars, and an over-hang on a wall will stop them from climbing over.

- The strongest block is obsidian—it won't be damaged by creeper explosions. If you don't have lots of rare obsidian to spare, build cobblestone walls that are five blocks high and three or four blocks deep. If you are short on cobblestone, make a cobblestone wall one block thick and use dirt or wood on the inside and outside. If you have no cobblestone, just use dirt or wood.

- Light up your roof to stop mobs spawning there. In fact, light up all your outside areas to minimize spawning.

- Because zombies can break through wood doors in Hard difficulty or Hardcore mode, use iron doors with buttons.

- Except for spiders, mobs can't cross a ditch that is one block wide and two blocks deep.

- Pour water into a ditch so that it flows to a trap or to an exit point. This way, mobs will flow from wherever they fall into the trap.

- Snow Golems will knock back mobs with their snowballs, and give some small damage to blazes and the Ender Dragon. Their snowballs will also cause Endermen to teleport. You can build a defensive barricade around your home filled with Snow Golems. It should be roofed so they aren't damaged by rain and fenced in so they don't wander. (Also, Snow Golems will melt in warmer biomes, like deserts.) You could also create mini guard towers for single Snow Golems, one or two blocks off the ground. To create a Snow Golem, place two snow blocks (made from four snowballs each) on top of each other on the ground and top with a pumpkin. Because Snow Golems attract hostile mobs, you can use them to lure mobs into a trap, such as a lava pit. Snow Golems can be killed by skeletons, and they don't attack creepers.

- In addition to tamed wolves, keep pet cats, to frighten creepers, and a pet Iron Golem, to attack any mobs.

- Because Endermen can teleport anywhere, build nooks inside and out that are only two blocks high (or two-and-a-half blocks high, by using slabs) that you can retreat to and fight them from.

## How Big?

Your house doesn't need to be huge. Most important is that it provides a safe place to sleep and use your stuff. So to start with, it needs to be big enough for your bed, your crafting table, a furnace, and a chest. As you progress, you'll want to have space for an enchanting table and bookshelves and a brewing station, as well as more furnaces and a lot more chests. If you are brewing a lot, you'll want a 2 × 2 well to get water from.

Probably the most important of all are your chests. If you mine, farm, and build a lot, you will end up needing many to store all your goods. One way to organize chests so that you can easily find everything quickly is keep all items of one type or category in separate chests. For example, all rare ore and metals in one chest, all building materials (cobblestone, fences) in another chest, and all plant material in another chest. You can place doubled-up chests above each other on a wall and place signs to say what's in them. (You can add four lines of text to a sign. To move up and down lines, use your up and down arrow keys.)

Make room for plenty of chests in your home, and make signs so you know what is where.

## Expanding

In addition to your shelter, as you expand you might want to add other types of structures to your home base—a map room to display your maps, a dock for your boats and for fishing, farms, and a watchtower or lookout. For extra protection, you can surround your home base with a massive stone wall. A helpful build near your home is a mob farm—one that just gathers and kills mobs for you, so you just need to retrieve their drops. Because mobs spawn at least twenty-four blocks away from you, you need to build your mob farm twenty-four blocks away from where you usually are—or twenty-four blocks or more in the air!

## Emergency Shelters

Sometimes you need a nighttime shelter, and fast. You know how to dig into a mountain and close it up for a quick shelter. You can also dig three blocks down and place dirt blocks above you. Or pillar jump with dirt or gravel blocks fifteen blocks up (to stay out of the range of skeleton arrows) and stay up there. If you carry a bed, dig out enough space or make a platform big enough for it so you can sleep through the night.

## Build a Simple Mob Farm

Mob farms are popular builds in Minecraft. Some mob farms are built to gather experience, like the zombie spawner farm explained in chapter 5. These gather mobs in one place so you can kill them and get the experience orbs. Other mob farms are built to automatically kill mobs and gather the loot they drop without giving you any experience—these contraptions are also called mob grinders. How fast a mob farm spawns and kills mobs depends on game mechanic factors like the conditions a mob will spawn in. For example, Endermen can only spawn in spaces that are three blocks high. Players have built hundreds of designs for mob farms and grinders. One of the simplest mob killing farms you can build is a closed-in, cobblestone room built twenty-eight blocks above the ground. (It is safest, and easiest, if you build this in Creative mode.) The reason to have this so high is that mobs spawn at least twenty-four blocks away from you. This farm also uses a long drop from the top to kill the mobs.[1]

(a) Build a 20×20 square floor, twenty-eight blocks up from ground level. This will be the base of the spawning chamber.

(b) Make a two-block-wide and two-block-deep trench from the center of one side to the opposite side, starting one block in from the outer edge. Dig an identical trench across the other side.

Partway done. The trenches that cross your spawning chamber should be two blocks deep and two blocks wide.

(c) In the middle of the crossing trenches, dig a 2 × 2 hole. (You can line the trenches with signs if you have them. Signs make mobs think that there is a block in the space. They trick the mob into walking into empty space where they will drop.)

(d) Now, at each of the four outer ends of the trenches, pour water against both corners of the outside wall blocks to make water flow along the trench towards the center. Because the trenches are eight blocks long, the water stops at the edge of the hole. This is where mobs will be pushed and drop. The drop to the ground (where you will place hoppers and chests to collect the drops) will kill them.

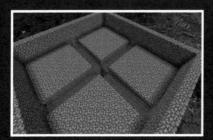

The spawning chamber is ready to be closed in.

(e) Build walls three blocks high around the base. Fill these in with a roof so you are leaving only two blocks of empty space in the spawning chamber.

(f) To know where to place the bottom collection point, build a 2 × 2 wall from one of the edges of the 2 × 2 hole down to the ground.

(g) Place two chests at the bottom of the wall and two hoppers above these, using Shift and right-clicking. In front of the two hoppers, place another two hoppers. The four hoppers need to be exactly underneath the 2 × 2 hole in the spawning chamber. Place four slabs on top of the hoppers, by pressing Shift and right-clicking.

On the ground directly beneath the spawning chamber's 4 × 4 hole, place two chests with four hoppers above.

(h) Now build out the chimney back up to the hole in the farm above. So you can see the mobs dropping and dying, use glass blocks at the bottom of the chimney.

The finished mob farm with the enclosed shaft. You can use glass at the bottom of the shaft to see your doomed mobs splat. Once the mobs start dropping, right-click on your chests to collect your loot.

Mob farms can be incredibly complex, and you can find many examples and tutorials online and on YouTube. Another popular structure to build is an automatic farm. These use pistons, redstone, and often water to automatically harvest your crop.

# CHAPTER 9
## FARMING

**F**arming is the best way in Minecraft to make sure you have a steady supply of food coming in. A farm also means you don't waste too much time hunting and gathering, so you can have more time for mining, exploring, and building. And it's fun, too! Once your seeds are planted and growing, the harvested food will provide enough seeds or starter crop for you to grow the next crop. While wheat is the most important crop, because it can make bread, try out all the different seeds. You can farm carrots, potatoes, melons, beetroot, pumpkins, and cocoa beans in pretty much the same way as wheat. It takes two to three days for a crop to fully grow. Once the crop is mature, you can leave it there until you are ready to collect it. When you are planning your farm, choose an area that is as flat as possible, and use your shovel to even the ground out. Make a shed to keep a crafting table and chest for farming supplies, like hoes and seeds, close by.

## Where to Find the Seeds

### Wheat
Break tall grass to gather wheat seeds. You use wheat to make bread, cookies, and cake, but you can also use it to lure and breed sheep and cows (and mooshrooms!).

**Carrots, Beetroot, and Potatoes**
You can find carrots, beetroot, and potatoes in village farms. Carrots and potatoes are sometimes dropped by zombies.

You can find carrots , beetroot, and potatoes in village farms.

Carrots and potatoes don't have seeds, you just plant the item and replant from your harvested crop. Watch out, though— every once in a while, a potato crop will give a poisonous potato. It has green patches on it, is a tiny bit smaller than a regular potato, and will poison you if you eat it. You can't cook it or plant it.

A poisonous potato (left) and a regular one (right).

### Melon and Pumpkin Seeds

You can find seeds in the chests of abandoned mineshafts. You can also buy them whole from villagers or find wild melons and pumpkins growing. Melons grow in jungles, while pumpkins grow in many biomes. When you plant them, first a stalk will grow, and then the fruit appears in a block next to the stalk.

You can find pumpkin growing in many biomes, but look for wild melons in the jungle. You can also find seeds in dungeon chests.

You will need to plant these seeds on farmland and make sure there are empty grass, dirt, or farmland blocks next to them. To harvest, gather the fruit only—leave the stem and it will grow more fruit! You can't use bone meal to grow a full pumpkin or melon. Bone meal will grow their stems though. The fastest way to harvest pumpkins and melons is with an axe.

## Don't Jump on the Farm!

Be careful when you are farming. Jumping on farmland can turn it back into dirt. Add fencing around plots, add pathways between crops or even raise up your garden.

A raised bed farm will help keep you from trampling the farmland.

## Faster and Better

To make your crops grow as fast as they can, make sure the farmland is watered and that your crops have light during the night. To water the farmland, there must be a source of water within four blocks. If you don't have a bucket yet to gather water, plant near a pond. One standard tactic is to make a 9 × 9 block of farmland with the center block dug out and filled with water. This leaves each farmland block within four blocks of water. Crops also grow faster if they are planted next to other types of crops. You don't need to make sure that each single plant is next to a different crop, just have rows of different crops next to each other.

Use a 9 × 9 block plot for the most efficient watering.

Crops mature to harvesting within three Minecraft days. You can make this closer to two days if the ground is watered, you plant in rows of different crops, you keep the edge of the farm plot as empty, watered farmland, and you keep the crops lit at night by placing torches on the surrounding fence.

If you have iron, you can make a bucket with three ingots. To get water from a river, lake, or sea, just right-click the bucket on the water. To make a never-ending supply of water, do the following: Dig a 2 × 2 hole, one block deep. Fill two corners opposite from each other with water. Now you can fill your bucket as many times as you need!

For an endless water supply, pour water into two opposite corners of a 2 × 2 hole.

## Close to Home

Because of the way memory is used in the programming of Minecraft, if you stray too far from home, the growth rate of your crops slows to nothing. So for the fastest growth, keep within a couple hundred blocks of your farm.

## When Is It Done?

Wheat is ready to harvest when the tops turn brown, and carrots are ready when you see the orange tops stick out. Potato is mature when you see the brown tops emerge. A melon or pumpkin is ready as soon as the melon or pumpkin block appears on an adjacent block.

As soon as a melon or pumpkin appears next to a stalk, it is ready to pluck.

## Sugar Cane Farm
------------------

You use sugar cane to make sugar for cake and pumpkin pie. But you also use it to make paper for maps and books, as well as fermented spider eyes and the Potion of Swiftness. It is an especially good way to trade with librarian villagers for emeralds. Build your own sugar cane farm so you have a steady supply for paper, maps, and books. You can find sugar cane on your travels growing alongside water.

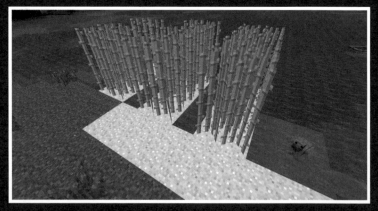

Sugar cane should be planted with one side next to water.

Since sugar cane doesn't have seeds, you will need to collect the sugar cane blocks and plant these. Sugar cane grows on sand, grass, or dirt, and the block needs to have at least one side next to water. One easy way to grow sugar cane is to plant rows, two blocks wide, into a pond. Leave one block of pond left between each row. This way, each sugar cane farm block is next to water. Sugar cane grows slowly to only three blocks high, even though wild sugar cane can grow higher. To harvest, you can break just the second block of the sugar cane—this will make both the second and third blocks fall, ready to collect. And this leaves the bottom block in place to grow more sugar cane.

## Cocoa Bean Farm

Cocoa beans grow in cocoa pods on jungle trees. Breaking a cocoa pod gives you a group of beans. To grow cocoa beans, you place blocks of jungle wood (it does not have to be a growing tree), then place cocoa beans on the side of this. Don't harvest cocoa pods until they mature and are colored orange-brown. Unripe cocoa pods only give one cocoa bean, and mature pods give two or three. You use cocoa to make brown dye, stain clay, glass, and wool brown, and make cookies and brown firework stars.

Grow cocoa beans on any blocks of jungle wood.

# CHAPTER 10
## FOOD AND FISHING

If you are playing in Survival mode on any difficulty beyond Peaceful, you will need to make sure you never get too hungry, because being too hungry drops your health points. (However, if you are playing on Easy or Normal levels, you won't die from starvation.) Both sprinting and jumping make you hungry. If your hunger goes below 6, you can't sprint. Eating something fills your hunger bar, and it is essential to rebuild your health, too. Also, when you are less hungry, you gain health more quickly.

## Saturation Point

In addition to the hunger bar, you also have a hidden score called "saturation," which depends on the type of food you have eaten. When your saturation isn't empty and you're not hungry, your health regenerates more quickly. Your hunger bar doesn't go down until your saturation reaches 0. You can tell your saturation level is at 0 when your hunger bar gets shaky, and that's when you'll start losing hunger points. Different activities can reduce your saturation level. Jumping while you sprint causes the biggest drop in saturation. Sneaking is half as exhausting as walking. Other actions that make the biggest hit on saturation include being poisoned, fighting, jumping, and sprinting. Different foods give you different saturation points and different hunger points. Cooking meat gives more saturation points. The top foods for hunger points are cake, rabbit stew, pumpkin pie, cooked porkchop, and steak. The top foods for saturation are golden carrot, porkchop, steak, and rabbit stew. Finally, the top four foods with the best overall food and saturation value rabbit stew, porkchop, steak, and golden carrot. Eating an entire cake will restore 14 hunger, but only give you 2.8 saturation, meaning it will fill you up but not very efficiently. The top overall? Rabbit stew, for 10 hunger points and 12 saturation. Make it with rabbit, mushroom, carrot, baked potato, and a bowl.

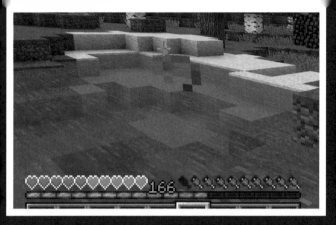

can be poisoned from eating pufferfish or spider eyes or by Witches or cave spi
son won't kill you but can drop you to half a heart. It will also make your screen
wave and your health and hunger bars go greenish.

## en Poison Is Good

In an emergency, you can eat raw chicken, rotten meat, and even spider eyes. They will give you poisoning, but you will recover f you are healthy. If you have milk from a cow to drink, you will recover faster. Eating a spider eye costs four damage points, but if you are desperate and need some hunger points to start healing, it can be a good solution.

## ok and Kill

You can cook your meat as you kill it, by lighting the ground an animal is on with flint and steel before you kill it. The animal will drop cooked meat instead of raw.

Firing up a cow before killing it will get you a cooked steak instead of raw.

## More Food Tips

- You can't eat cake unless it's been placed on a block.

- Eating several raw chickens will give you more hunger points than the poisoning can take away.

- If you eat while moving, you slow down. However, you can eat on a ladder without slowing down.

- To milk a cow, hold a bucket and right-click the cow.

- Mooshrooms supply mushroom stew instead of milk. If you have a mooshroom, you have an endless supply of stew. To milk (or mushroom stew) a mooshroom, hold a bowl and right-click it.

- If you know you'll be fighting, eat the foods with the greatest value: rabbit stew, porkchop, steak, and golden carrot. Take them into combat with you, too, to eat when recovering from damage.

## Fishing for Food

Rainy day? You can sleep in your bed during a thunderstorm, even if it isn't night! Or better yet, fish—there are more fish during rain than when it's clear. Ordinarily, fishing outside will get you a fish in less than forty-five seconds. If it's raining, your chances improve by about 20 percent.

Craft a fishing rod from sticks and string, and right-click on water while holding the rod to cast the line. Watch the bobber. When a fish is ready to bite, you will see a small trail of bubbles. When the bobber dips below the water, right-click to bring the line and fish in. The fish will fly at you, sometimes over your head, before it drops to the ground. Often it will fly straight into your inventory.

Right before a fish bites, you'll see a trail of bubbles. When the bobber dips, the fish

Sometimes you can catch treasure or junk with the fishing rod. Fishing treasure can be saddles, lily pads, name tags, enchanted but used bows and fishing rods, and enchanted books. Fishing can also bring you junk—stuff like bowls, leather, squid ink sacs, leather boots, sticks, string, damaged bows and fishing rods, trip wire hooks, water bottles, and bones. So sometimes you might want junk! With an enchanted rod, you have a greater chance of catching treasure instead of junk.

## Beyond Fishing

You can use your fishing rod to hook other entities, like mobs. Drag a zombie into lava! Drag a skeleton over a cliff! Hooking a mob with a fishing rod counts as an attack and will drop the durability of the rod. However, hooking them by itself doesn't actually do them any damage.

## More Fishing Tips

- A fishing rod can be used sixty-five times before it breaks.

- With a regular fishing rod, you have a 10 percent chance of catching junk and a 5 percent chance of catching treasure.

- Fishing lowers in durability when you hit a solid block, under water or on ground, or an entity.

- Endermen will teleport if you hook them but will still be hooked.

- If you are desperate for food, create your own pool of water from a 2×2 dug-out square. Fill it with water from the bucket of water you have stored, and fish in that!

- You can also fish in waterfalls.

**You can make your own water hole to fish in, or even fish in a waterfall.**

- You can use a fishing rod to pull a mob to a height. When the mob falls from a high enough level, it will be killed.

- Fish in a boat to get a break from mobs.

- You can fish inside and underground, but it will take about double the time to catch a fish.

- You don't have to stay absolutely still while fishing—you can move about thirty-five blocks from the bobber.

# CHAPTER II

# ENCHANTING AND POTIONS

**E**nchanting your weapons gives you an extra edge, which can mean the difference between life and death, and enchanting your mining tools lets you take home double the loot in half the time! There are a couple ways to enchant your tools, weapons, and armor. You can use an enchantment table or an anvil, or you can trade with a villager for an already enchanted item or book. Enchanting costs experience points (XP) and a little lapis.

Besides trading with a village priest, you enchant your tools and weapons through an enchantment table or an anvil.

## An Enchanting Experience

Experience points (XP) are the main currency for enchanting, and you get XP (the floating green orbs) from doing things like killing mobs (other than baby animals, golems, bats, and villagers), mining (other than iron and gold), smelting and cooking with the furnace, fishing, trading, and breeding. Experience points fill up your experience bar, and when the bar is filled, you gain a new level. Then the bar is empty again and ready to fill for the next level. Above level 15, you need increasing XP at each level to reach the next. Experience points are only used for enchanting and the anvil. Make sure to pick up all the orbs you see, as any that aren't collected in five minutes disappear.

The floating green orbs that appear after you complete some activities, like killing a mob, add up to the experience levels you need to use the enchantment table and anvil. This experience bar is at level 74.

## An Enchanting Village

You can buy enchanted items from villagers: armor from armorers, axes and swords from weapon smiths, picks from tool smiths, rods from fishermen, and books from librarians.

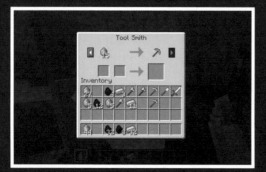

You can buy enchanted tools, weapons, armor, and more from villagers.

## The Enchantment Table

Right-click an enchantment table to open the Enchant screen. Under the open book are two slots. In the left you place the item to be enchanted. In the right you place 1 to 3 lapis. On the right of the screen are three buttons that show three possible enchants for your item. The top button is an enchant you can get with 1 lapis, the middle will need 2 lapis, and the bottom will need 3. In addition to lapis, you will need to have a certain number of experience points to get an enchant. This is shown by the green number on each button. To know what the enchant will be and exactly what it will cost, mouse over the enchant button. It shows the enchant, the lapis amount, and the number of XP levels you will lose. You will only be shown one enchant per button however. Once you click the enchant button to place the enchant, you may get more!

When you choose an enchantment with the enchantment table, you will only know one enchantment. You may actually end up getting two or more enchants.

The more bookshelves that are placed around the enchantment table, the stronger the enchantment choices, and the more costly. You can put up to fifteen bookshelves around an enchantment table. There must be a block of space between the bookshelves and the enchantment table, and the bookshelves must be at the same height or one above the table. If you have placed so many bookshelves that you now don't have enough XP to buy at the high level of enchantments, you can disable the effect by placing torches on the side of the bookshelves facing the table.

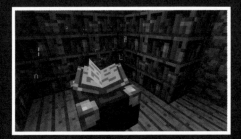

To strengthen your enchantment table, place bookshelves around it, two blocks away. You'll see the magic symbols float from the shelves to the book on the enchantment table.

You can disable the strengthening effect of a bookshelf by placing a torch on it.

## The Anvil

With an anvil you can:

- Combine two enchanted items to create an undamaged third item with both enchantments. The item in the left slot is the target, and the item in the right slot is "sacrificed." The two initial items must have compatible enchantments. If one of the initial items is damaged, then the cost will increase, but the total cost can't be more than 39 XP.

With an anvil, the two items you are repairing must have compatible enchantments.

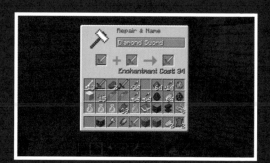

- Enchant an item with the enchantment of an enchanted book. The enchanted book goes in the second slot.

You can enchant an item with an enchanted book. Hover over the rightmost slot to see what the final enchantment will bring.

- Repair an item with blocks of the same raw material it is made of. The raw material goes into the second slot.
- Rename an item. Renaming also costs XP. Renaming can also make it easier for you to find a favorite pickaxe!

- Use a Mending enchantment. Found when looting chests, fishing, or trading for enchanted books, the Mending enchantment can be used to fix weapons and armor as you gain XP. Place the item to be enchanted in the left slot and the enchantment in the right. As you run into XP while holding the enchanted item in either hand or wearing the armor, the XP will repair it instead of going into your XP bar. Since hostile mobs drop twice as much XP as tame or neutral mobs, your weapon will charge more quickly in battle.

- Use the Frost Walker enchantment. A treasure enchantment similar to Mending, Frost Walker turns the blocks around you into ice. Frost Walker I gives you a small radius while higher numbers surround you with larger ice patches. The ice does melt quickly— more quickly in daylight than at night—so don't stay in one place for more than a couple of seconds!

Right-click to open an anvil. It will show your inventory, and there will be two slots you use. You place the item to repair in the left slot and the matching item (which you will sacrifice), or raw material (like iron) in the second. The repaired item shows in the slot at the far right. The repair will cost experience points. A tool tip will show the enchantments the repaired item will have. To see its durability, press F3+H. If both items you place are enchanted and the enchantments are compatible, the repaired item will have both enchantments.

## Get More Experience

You get the most experience points from killing hostile mobs (especially those with armor), breaking a bottle o' enchanting (which you can get from a village priest), and from destroying mob spawners. You get a massive number of points for killing the Ender Dragon (12,000 XP) and fifty from killing a Wither. Fast ways to get more experience points quickly are mob experience (XP) farms and mining Nether quartz for experience. You can also breed animals quickly, killing and cooking their meat as you go.

## More Enchanting and Anvil Tips

- Don't repair an enchanted item on your crafting table. This will remove any enchantment. Use the anvil instead.

- The more you enchant an item, the more expensive in XP levels it gets. After a while (about 6 times) it will be too expensive to enchant.

- Reverse the order of two items in the anvil. This can sometimes make an enchant cheaper.

- Name tags are found in chests in dungeons and by fishing. You can rename them in the anvil and attach them to a mob.

- If you enchant books (or find them), you can build a library of books enchanted with different effects. Then you can choose to add a specific enchantment to an item by using the anvil.

- Anvils are damaged the more they are used. You can use an anvil about twenty-four times before it is very damaged and disappears.

When an anvil is very damaged and about to break, its surface looks spotted.

- An item can only have one type of protection enchantment and one type of damage enchantment at a time. It can't have two versions of the same enchantment, either.

## Potions

Potions are very powerful. You brew them with a brewing station using rare ingredients. They grant you a specific power or ability, like breathing underwater, being fire resistant, or moving very fast for a certain amount of time. Witches sometimes drop potions when you kill them, but to have a reliable source of potions you will need to brew them yourself. To do this, you must have some ingredients you can only find in the Nether. You will need a blaze rod in order to craft the brewing stand. To get a blaze rod, you will need to kill a mob called the blaze, which lives in Nether fortresses.

In addition, most potions use Nether wart. You find Nether wart growing around staircases in Nether fortresses. It only grows on Soul Sand, also found in the Nether, but doesn't need light or water. Since you will need a supply of this, make your own farm by bringing back Nether wart and soul sand from a trip to the Nether.

For a potion-brewing setup, have at the ready your brewing stand, a water supply, a furnace for making glass bottles, blaze powder, and a supply of Nether warts. You'll need one piece of blaze powder for every twenty ingredients you place in the brewing stand.

To begin brewing potions, right-click the brewing station.

**Primary Potions**

Once you have filled bottles with water, you brew these with another ingredient to make a base or primary potion. Primary potions don't do anything themselves, but you brew them with other ingredients to create your final potion. You add Nether wart for the Awkward potion, glowstone dust for the Thick potion, and fermented spider eye for the potion of Weakness. For the Mundane potion, you add one of the following: ghast tears, glistering melon, blaze powder, magma cream, sugar, or spider eye. You use redstone for the Mundane potion (extended time).

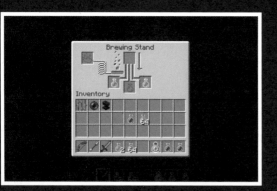

To make a potion, place blaze powder in the top left slot to fuel the brewing station. Place glass bottles filled with water in the bottom slots and your added ingredient in the top slot. You don't have to fill all bottle slots, but if you don't you will waste ingredients.

### Secondary Potions

Once you have a primary potion, you brew this with another ingredient for a secondary potion that you can use. The Awkward potion is the base for most secondary potions. With the Awkward potion, add magma cream for Fire Resistance, glistering melon for Healing, golden carrot for Night Vision, ghast tear for Regeneration, blaze powder for Strength, sugar for Swiftness, rabbit's foot for Leaping, and pufferfish for Water Breathing. For a potion of Weakness, add the fermented spider eye to any of the base potions, and for a potion of Poison, add spider eye to the Awkward potion.

### Tertiary Potions

You can make new potions from these secondary potions. Add gunpowder to turn the potion into a splash potion, glowstone dust to make the potion twice as strong (and sometimes lose duration), and redstone to make the effect last twice as long. You can use fermented eye of spider to "corrupt" the effect, or make it do the opposite. For example, add the fermented eye of spider to a Potion of Swiftness to make it a potion of Slowness.

### Lingering Potions

Add dragon's breath to any splash potion to create a lingering potion that hovers like a cloud. This is effective when disabling hostile mobs, helping your allies, and creating multiple tipped arrows at one time.

### More Potion Tips

- Combine a potion with gunpowder to turn it into a splash potion you can throw at your own feet or the feet of your enemy.

- To use a potion, you right-click with it in your hand. To see what potions you currently have active, open your inventory.

- For efficient brewing, always brew three bottles. One ingredient is enough to brew all three.

- You can add a single ingredient to three different types of potions. For example, you can brew three different splash potions by combining gunpowder with a potion of Poison, a potion of Weakness, and a potion of Harming in one brewing session. Dragon's breath can create lingering potions of Luck and Strength for you and your allies and a lingering potion of Slowness to disable your enemies, all in one brewing session.

- Using gunpowder for a splash potion makes it 25 percent less strong, and the shape of the bottle will change to a round shape with a handle, a bit like a grenade.

- Throwing a harming potion at a zombie or skeleton actually helps them heal (because they are undead to begin with!). Splash them with a healing potion instead.

- To fill a bottle, hold it and right-click a water source. Filling a water bottle from a water-filled cauldron will drain the cauldron by a third, so use a water supply you make yourself.

- The brewing station will show you the name of the final potion and its effect when you place a base potion and an ingredient into its slots.

- Because gathering the ingredients for potions is dangerous, use enchanting instead to help you while you hone your skills. When you are ready for trips back and forth from the Nether, you are ready for potions!

## Tipped Arrows

Arrows can be tipped with lingering potion to deliver a status effect to a target. Status effects delivered include Luck, Bad Luck, Strength, Weakness, Invisibility, Night Vision, Water Breathing and seven others. You can craft up to eight at a time by placing the arrows around the lingering potion in the crafting table. You can also create a spectral arrow using glowstone dust to highlight your target so you can see it in the dark or when it's hiding. Your status effects are visible in the heads-up display instead of in your inventory.

# CHAPTER 12

## UNDERSTANDING REDSTONE

Redstone is a powerful ore in Minecraft that allows you to make automatic contraptions like automatic sliding doors, elevators, and farms that harvest your wheat automatically.

An iron door is one of the simplest redstone contraptions. The device is the iron door, and it is activated (opened) by a power signal from the pressure plate on a neighboring block.

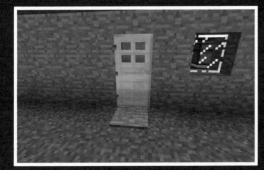

Redstone is a little bit like electricity. It is a power source, and you use redstone wire like an electric wire, sending power signals to an object or device to do something like open a door. A redstone contraption needs at least two things—redstone power source and the device itself. It can also have a third element for transmitting the power longer distances.

- **The device:** Redstone devices are items that respond to a redstone power signal by doing something. Devices include dispensers (which eject items), doors (which can be opened remotely), and pistons (which can move blocks).

- **The power source:** To get the device to react, you need to activate it with a power source. The power signal comes from a special item either made from redstone or programmed to give a signal. You can place the power source right next to the device to power it. Types of power sources include a redstone torch, a button, and a lever. A lever or button might seem like a type of device, but they actually produce a redstone signal that activates devices.

- **Power transmission:** If you want or need to place the power source further away from the device, you can use redstone wire to transmit the power. This means you can place a lever three blocks away from a piston and connect the two with redstone wire. Signals are also carried by two other items: comparators and repeaters.

## A Simple Contraption: the Iron Door

A working iron door is one of the simplest redstone contraptions. Iron doors only open with a signal. Place your iron door in a wall of your home. Put a pressure plate directly in front of it. To open the door, stand on the pressure plate. Doing this makes the power source—the pressure plate—transmit a redstone signal to the door. The door—a device—is programmed to react to the signal by opening. However, if the door is an exterior door, don't use a pressure plate on the outside. A mob could stand on it by accident and get into your house. Put a button on the wall outside.

There are many types of power sources, devices, and ways to modify a power signal traveling along a wire. There are special rules that govern how each item acts and reacts. It gets pretty complicated, and creating redstone contraptions is one of the hardest things to do in Minecraft.

A great way to start working with and understanding redstone is to explore it and make machines, from simple to complex, in Creative mode. In Creative mode, you have access to all the types of blocks you need, without having to craft them. Put a power source next to a device that can be activated, like a lever next to a door, and see what happens. Search online for tutorials on building redstone mechanisms and follow them. First, learn what the different devices, power sources, and signal modifiers are.

## Devices

- **Dispenser:** A dispenser ejects items in the same way a player drops items. However, if the item is a projectile, the dispenser will fire it. Some dispensed items are also activated (as when a player right-clicks an item). These items include minecarts (if there's a rail in front of the dispenser), boats (if there is water), TNT, bone meal, flint, steel, water buckets, and lava buckets. If you put these items in a dispenser they'll come out ready to go, so you can use dispensers to fill your moat with lava with a push of a button, remotely detonate TNT, or deploy a fleet of carts for your roller coaster from the control booth!

- **Doors:** These include iron doors, wood doors, fence gates, and trap doors. The only one of these that must have a power signal in order to work is an iron door, but you can power other doors, too. This way you can open your fence gates with a push of a button (they close quickly behind you to keep your animals from following), or open the doors inside your house with pressure plates. You can even make a trap door to drop you to the next floor with the flip of a switch!

- **Dropper:** Droppers drop items stored inside them to the floor or to a container that has an inventory, like a hopper or chest, in front of it.

- **Hopper:** A hopper transfers items between containers, including chests and minecarts. It can transfer items in its own small inventory of five items or items in a container placed above it. It transfers the items to containers placed below its output. Powering a hopper stops this activity.

- **Minecart rails:** These include powered rails, activator rails, and detector rails.

- **Note block:** When a note block receives a power signal or a player clicks it, it plays a musical note, F-sharp. You can right-click a note block to make it a higher pitch.

- **Piston and sticky piston:** When powered, a piston block expands to occupy two blocks, pushing the block in front of it one block away. A sticky piston can retract as well. You can use pistons to make all kinds of creations, like a castle drawbridge or a hidden cave door.

- **Redstone lamp:** A redstone lamp can be turned on by power. It is a little brighter than a torch, and it looks a bit more fashionable.

- **TNT:** You can detonate a block of TNT by powering it.

Redstone devices include doors, droppers, hoppers, power and activator rails, note blocks, pistons and sticky pistons, redstone lamps, and TNT.

## Power Sources

Some power sources are always "on," or always transmitting power, and others need to be turned on like a switch. They provide power to themselves (the block space they are "in") and to the blocks they are attached to. Some power sources also power the blocks next to the block they are attached to. These include buttons, detector rails, levers, pressure plates, and trip wire hooks.

- **Observer:** An observer watches the block directly in front of it, and sends a redstone pulse out its back if that block changes. The types of changes it recognizes include crops growing, piston heads moving, redstone item changes, and opening of chests.

- **Redstone torch:** This provides power constantly, to itself and to the block above it, rather than the block it is placed on. However, if the block that the redstone torch is attached to gets powered or switched on separately by another block, the redstone torch will turn off.

- **Redstone block:** Like a redstone torch, redstone is always on. Unlike a redstone torch, it cannot be switched off. It cannot power the block above it, it only powers itself.

- **Lever:** In the "on" position, a lever provides power to the block it is attached to.

- **Button:** Pressing a stone button gives power for one second (a wood button 1.5 seconds) to itself and the block it is attached to. Wooden buttons can be pressed by arrows, which keep the button depressed.

- **Pressure plates:** Stone or wood pressure plates provide power for one second, or for the time an item is on it. Pressure plates are activated by players, mobs, or a minecart with a mob in it. Wooden plates can also be activated by arrows, fishing rod lures, any minecart, and any dropped items. A pressure plate powers the block beneath it.

- **Weighted pressure plates:** Gold and iron pressure plates provide an amount of power that depends on the weight of items dropped on them. Gold produces less power per item than iron.

- **Detector rail:** A detector rail provides a power signal when a minecart is on it. Detector rails are often used to switch the tracks a minecart is on.

- **Trip wire hooks:** Two trip wire hooks power the blocks they are attached to when the string that attaches them to each other is stood on or walked over (by a player, for example). Two trip wire hooks can be up to forty blocks apart.

- **Trapped chest:** You craft a trapped chest from a trip wire hook and chest. When the chest is opened, it produces a weak power to the block it is placed on and itself.

- **Daylight sensor:** Daylight sensors provide an amount of power that depends on the amount of daylight, so they are strongest at noon.

- **Containers:** Containers (with inventories) like brewing stands, chests, dispensers, droppers, furnaces, hoppers, and jukeboxes provide a power signal to a comparator. The signals they emit grow stronger the more items they contain, relative to the total amount they are able to store. This means that a container with twenty-seven slots but only three items will send a weaker signal than a container with five slots and three items.

Redstone power sources transmit a redstone signal to a device. The signal may be temporary, as with a button, or constant, as with a redstone torch. They include redstone torches and redstone blocks, levers, buttons, pressure plates and weighted pressure plates, detector rails, daylight sensors, and trip wire hooks.

## Transmitting Power

To connect a power source that is a block or more away from the device, you will need to use redstone wire. You can modify the redstone signal with a repeater or a comparator.

- **Redstone wire:** Redstone wire carries power from a power source for fifteen blocks. The signal weakens as it travels. You can tell redstone wire is carrying power if it lights up and is sparkling. The redstone wire gives power to the block beneath it and the block that the end of the wire is attached to.

(Redstone "occupies" the block above the block that it is sitting on.)

- **Redstone repeater:** Redstone repeaters allow redstone wire to carry the signal longer than fifteen blocks. A repeater increases the power signal to its original strength and lets it travel another fifteen blocks. Repeaters also cause a delay in the signal. You can set the delay to .1, .2, .3, or .4 seconds. Power can only pass through a repeater in one direction, from the back to the front, marked by a faint triangle or arrow.

- **Comparator:** A comparator looks a bit like a repeater but it does something different. It compares the signal coming to it from the back to the signal coming to it from the side. (The front is marked the same way as a repeater, with an arrow.) If the signal from the back is greater than the signal from the side, it will send the back signal power out the front; otherwise, it will send no signal. A comparator can also act in a "subtract" mode, which you activate by right-clicking it. In subtract mode, it compares the two signals, then subtracts the amount of power coming from the side and then sends the rest forward. If the side power is greater than the back, no signal is sent.

In changing the signal being transmitted, you use redstone wire (to carry the signal for fifteen blocks), redstone repeaters (to help the signal carry longer than fifteen blocks), and comparators (to modify a signal based on a second signal's input).

## Timing Is Everything

One thing to be aware of when building complicated contraptions is that many of these blocks react with small delays in timing, called ticks. For example a redstone torch takes one tick (.1 seconds) to change from on to off. This means that complicated machines may not work as you expect, because there are too many delays. You need to be careful about timing, and if you are having a problem, you can research the items you are using online to see what advanced features and side effects they have that may be causing the problem. Creating machines and circuits with redstone gets to be very advanced—like studying electronics. You can read more about all of these elements online. A great place to start is the Minecraft wiki, at minecraft.gamepedia.com.

## Powered Blocks

Most solid blocks, like cobblestone, that you can't see through can be powered. A powered block doesn't transmit power to the blocks next to it, but it can activate a device it is next to. This is what happens when you push a button on a block next to an iron door. See-through blocks, like glass or leaves, typically can't be powered.

## Cobblestone Piston Doors

Pistons and sticky pistons are used in many redstone contraptions because they move the block immediately in front of them. They are used in contraptions to harvest farm crops, kill mobs, move elevators, and make sliding doors. Follow these steps for a set of automatic sliding piston doors.

(a) Place four cobblestone blocks, two wide and two high, to make the doors.

(b) On the side of the door, place two sticky pistons stacked on top of each other, one block away from the door. (When you place a piston, the moving slab faces you.)

Create two cobblestone doors out of four cobblestone blocks. Add two sets of two sticky pistons, one block away on each side.

(c) Place a redstone torch with a cobblestone block on top, on the other side of the two sticky piston stacks. The redstone torch activates the bottom piston. It also powers the cobblestone above it, which activates the top sticky piston.

Power the pistons. The bottom one is activated by a redstone torch. The top piston is activated by the same redstone torch signal, passed through the cobblestone block above the torch.

These three steps create a piston door that is shut, because the power from the redstone torch—which is always on—keeps the pistons extended. But you need to have the doors open to get through them, of course! So you need a way to power off the redstone torch powering the pistons. Luckily, whenever a redstone torch has power sent to it, it turns off! To do this, you can use pressure plates that will send a power signal over redstone wire to the redstone torches. The four pressure plates (two on either side of the door) will be placed two blocks away from the doors.

(d)  Dig two trenches two blocks deep on each side to connect the side of the redstone torch with the pressure plates. However, at the redstone torch, you will need to place one block as a step to reach it. This is because redstone wire can't climb up more than one block at a time, so you use stepped blocks to raise the wire. The trench must be two blocks deep, because redstone needs a free block above it in order to work. (You can use a slab in place of a block to cover redstone, as this leaves space for the redstone to work.)

(e)  When the trenches are dug, place redstone wire along them from one end to the other.

Dig trenches to run redstone wire from one end to the other.

(f) On both sides of the door, replace the empty blocks directly in front of the doors with wood planks or another flooring material, and place your pressure plates on these.

Add dirt blocks in front of the doors and stone pressure plates along these.

You should now be able to pass through the doors. As you walk on the pressure plates, they give power to the redstone wire beneath them that travels to the sticky pistons and turns them off. This makes the doors open. By the time you pass through the doors, the pressure plates turn off, closing the doors. Now you can cover up the trenches and wiring with any building blocks you like. Remember that you must leave a block of space above each block with placed redstone wire. If the redstone wire is traveling up the side of a block, it is the top of that block that needs a full block of space above it.

This is the finished door, with the sliding door mechanisms completely covered up.

# CHAPTER 13

## RAILWAYS

Whether you need to traffic loads of ore from your mines back to your base, or you just want a quick way to travel to all the villages you are saving, minecart railways are a perfect way to speed up your journeys. Except for horses (and flying in Creative mode), they're the fastest way to get around. You can build them up, around, or through mountains and down to the bottommost mines, cross lakes, and stop along the way at stations you can trick out any way you like. You aren't safe from mobs while you're traveling though. Even a sheep can get in the way and derail you. The safest railways are underground, in lit corridors that mobs can't spawn in, or elevated. If you are building an elevated railway, make sure to keep it lit and well away from trees and other blocks that mobs can jump from.

Build an elevated railway to steer clear of mobs, but make sure to keep it lit!

## Types of Minecarts

As well as the standard minecart you ride in, you can also create a powered minecart (a minecart with a furnace), which can push carts in front of it; a storage minecart (cart with a chest); and a hopper minecart (a cart with a hopper). Hopper minecarts gather items on the track or can be loaded from other containers. Minecarts don't attach to each other, but one can push the others in front.

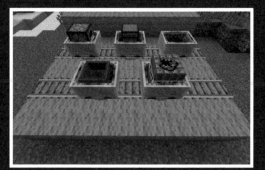

As well as the regular minecart you can hop in yourself, there's a powered minecart, storage minecart, hopper minecart, and TNT minecart.

## Types of Rails

Along with the regular rails, there are three types of rails that perform specific duties:

- **Powered rails:** Activate these with a redstone torch or they will bring the cart to a stop. A redstone torch will activate the powered rail it is attached to and up to eight additional powered rails following it. Powered rails can also be activated by detector rails, powered redstone wire, a lever, or by being placed on a redstone block.

- **Detector rails:** Detector rails act like a pressure plate. They give out a power signal when a cart is over them to their neighboring blocks. You can use these to power powered rails, activate note blocks to signal a train is coming, activate dispensers to drop items or shoot arrows, or switch tracks at a T junction.

- **Activator rails:** When powered, these can do two things: activate or deactivate a hopper minecart, or activate a TNT minecart.

The four types of rails are regular rails, powered rails, detector rails, and activator rails.

## Simple Railway System

You can easily build a one-track railway system with stops on the way and two simple endpoints. Power your railway starts by digging a 2 × 1 hole and using powered rails. The very last rail at the endpoint should have a button that you press to get going.

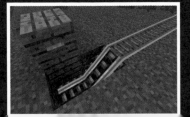

This simple endpoint stop uses two powered rails and a button to power the last powered rail.

For in-between stops, dig a 2 × 1 hole that has two powered rails in the hole, also powered with a button. This will bring your cart to a stop, then you press the button to move forward in the direction you are going.

The simplest in-between stop has two powered rails and a button.

Another simple in-between stop uses a raised 2 × 1 platform with regular rails on top. At either end of the platform, place two powered rails leading to the platform and, next to these, detector rails. Connect buttons with redstone wire to the rising powered rails on either side. The detector rails power your movement up to the platform, and the buttons power you forward. (If your button doesn't seem to be working, make sure you are on the powered rail that is sloping. You can adjust your position slightly by pressing W.)

Another type of in-between stop uses a platform, four powered rails, two detector rails, and two buttons. Here, the buttons are connected to the powered rails by redstone wire.

## Roller Coasters

Build a fantastic roller coaster by using cobblestone, wood planks, or other blocks to make your base for the rails. Place rails on the ramps, adding plenty of powered rails to help your minecart go up slopes. End the rollercoaster where you started. To build a simple stop, place two powered rails, the first on a descending block and the second on a level block. Place a button on a wall beside the descending block. When your cart reaches the descending block, it will brake. You can start it forward again by pressing the button. (You must be on the descending block while pressing the button.)

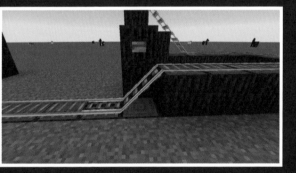

This rollercoaster uses another type of stop. Notice the button powers the sloping powered rail.

There are two main rules for how powering a powered rail helps a stationary minecart start moving again.

(1) If there is a block at one end of the powered rail, the minecart will be moved in the opposite direction.

(2) If the powered rail is on a slope, the minecart will be moved down the slope.

Rails aren't just for transporting ore. Build a rollercoaster high in the sky.

## Full Speed Ahead

Some Minecraft players timed the speeds and effects of powered rails. Their results showed that for full speed on a level surface (for an occupied cart), place a powered rail every thirty-four blocks. Other studies say to put two powered rails every thirty-seven blocks. Going up a slope, put a powered rail every four blocks. For an unoccupied cart, you'll need a powered rail every seven blocks. Uphill, place powered rails every two blocks for occupied carts and every block for unoccupied carts.

## More Tips on Rails

- Minecarts move faster when a player is in them than when they are empty.

- Use a pickaxe to break up rails fastest.

- Occasionally, a curved rail that is placed correctly will look like it is curving in the wrong direction. Test it with a cart to see if it is working.

- Your minecart will travel faster on "diagonal" rails—rails that curve in one direction for one block, then another, continuously.

Curving rails left and right with each block creates diagonal rails. Your cart will travel in a straight line down the diagonal, with increased speed.

- At intersections where tracks cross each other but aren't curved, minecarts will always take whichever direction is downhill. If all directions are level, then the cart will turn either to the south or to the east.

- You can also put TNT in a minecart and activate the blast with a powered activator rail, fire, lava, a collision, or by dropping over three blocks.

- Only regular rails can be used at a curve or a T junction.

- You can't place a powered rail at a curve.

# CHAPTER 14

# GETTING CREATIVE

**T**he block is the basic building unit in Minecraft, and Minecraft blocks are designed to be stacked, combined, and rearranged in an endless number of ways to create just about anything you can think of. While you can build working devices, contraptions, railways, clothes, tools, and other useful things, you can also use blocks just to be creative. Make two-dimensional pixel art with Minecraft's colored blocks.

Make pixel art with Minecraft's colored blocks.

Build the Minecraft version of your own home, create a medieval castle, or sculpt a mountain into Godzilla. Minecraft players have built (singly or in teams) incredible models of real-life palaces, cities, and national monuments, from the Empire State Building to the Taj Mahal. If building is your thing, there's lots you can do!

Your first Minecraft home was probably a simple square or a hole dug into a mountain. But if you have an architectural streak, there's no limit to the styles and sizes of homes and buildings you can create, with all of the building and textured blocks the game offers. To get started improving your house design:

- Use two types of contrasting blocks for your main structures. You can use one of the block types for corners and edges, as accent. For a modern look, try stone (not cobblestone) and light wood planks. For a country look, use cobblestone and wood planks. Mix light and dark wood, planks and raw wood. Bring in colored walls by using stained (dyed) clay, like a green clay, and pair it with sandstone.

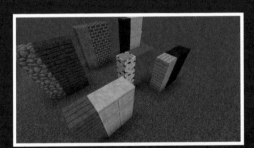

One way to make a house stand out is to use contrasting blocks and textures.

For a great, simple look, use two different types of blocks. This house uses the stone block and the dark oak wood block as well as leaf blocks for edging. You can use slabs to build up the slopes of a roof.

With dyed clay blocks, you can make very colorful buildings and structures.

- Add details: chimneys, hedges made from leaf blocks, ponds, fountains, and pathways. Use slabs to build up peaked roofs.

Add chimneys, hedges, and landscaping details to your homes.

- Get inspiration! Look online and in books for houses and styles you'd like to build. Build a towering castle with turrets, a pagoda, a treehouse with winding treetop paths, a modern beachside home, or massive military barracks!

- Leave the tiny 1×1 windows behind. Add wide windows, floor to ceiling windows, even skylights. In traditional houses, use trap doors for shutters.

- Use slabs to make different levels of floor inside.

Players have discovered many inventive ways to use Minecraft blocks for home design, furniture, and décor. There are some built-in home decoration items: paintings, carpet, flowerpots, glass panes, and item frames. When you place a painting on a wall, you'll randomly get one of twenty-six Minecraft paintings, in sizes $1 \times 1$ up to $4 \times 4$. The block where you place the painting will be the painting's bottom left corner.

Even though Minecraft doesn't include chairs and table and other furniture, players have been using existing blocks to add furniture and more to their homes. Experiment with combining blocks with fences, fence gates, signs, stair blocks, slabs, pressure plates, trap doors, pistons, glowstone, dyed wool, glass, and buttons. A stair block with two signs on its sides is a chair!

Some classic combinations are:

- Chairs and sofas: Use stairs or slabs, with signs or trap doors for arms.

- Tables: Use fence block with pressure plates above.

- Lamps: Fence block with glowstone, surrounded by trap doors.

- Fireplace: Place Netherrack within nonflammable blocks like stone, and light for an inside roaring fire. (Make sure the fire is not within 2 blocks of flammable material like wood.)

Make sofas and chairs from stairs, and use trapdoors and signs for arms. Use a slab for a coffee table. You can make a floor lamp with fencing, glowstone, and trap doors, and a TV from black wool and a painting.

## Dyeing for Color

There are sixteen dyes you can make in Minecraft, and you can use the dyes to color wool, sheep, terracotta, leather armor, banners, concrete, and glass. Some dyes you make by placing a flower of the same color on a crafting grid: Rose Red (poppy, rose bush, red tulip, beetroot), Orange, Dandelion Yellow, Light Blue (orchid), Magenta (lilac, allium), Pink, Light Gray (white tulip, oxeye daisy, azure bluet). For Cactus Green, smelt a cactus; for Lapis Lazuli dye (a deep blue), use the lapis lazuli ore; and for White, use bone meal. Use a squid ink sac for Black and cocoa beans for Cocoa Bean (brown). You can also make four other dyes: Lime (cactus green and bone meal), Gray (bone meal and ink sac), Cyan (cactus green and lapis lazuli), Purple (lapis lazuli and red). For a constant supply of dyed wool, dye a sheep. You can also combine dyes with glass for stained glass and with terracotta (created by smelting clay or from the Mesa biome) for colored terracotta. You can then smelt dyed terracotta to create amazing glazed terracotta patterns.

You can make sixteen dyes using plants and other items, and they can be used to color wool (and sheep), glass, and hardened clay.

## Fireworks!

Make colorful explosions in the sky with fireworks. Fireworks can only be crafted—they are not in the Creative mode inventory. To create an exploding firework, first make a colored firework star using gunpowder and a dye. Add a diamond in the crafting screen to add trails or glowstone dust to add a twinkle. You can also change the shape of the explosion from a sphere. For a larger sphere, add a fire charge; for a star shape, add a gold nugget. Add a feather for a burst and any mob head for a creeper head shape. Then, to make the final firework rocket, combine your fireworks star with one paper and one gunpowder. Add one or two more gunpowder for greater height and more firework stars for more explosions! Set these off outside by right-clicking to place them.

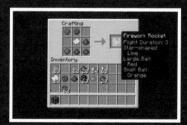

Create fireworks with firework stars, gunpowder, and paper. What you add to a firework star determines its shape, color, and special effects like trails, and you

## Consider Creative Mode

If you are planning an extensive build, and the glory of battling mobs isn't a priority, work in Creative mode. In Creative mode, you have access to all of Minecraft's blocks, from cyan wool to decorative mob heads. You don't need tools—you can destroy blocks with your hand or any other item except a sword. And you can fly! Press the spacebar twice to start flying; then press space to rise higher and shift to lower. You won't get hungry or be damaged if you fall, so you have all the time you need to make whatever you want.

Also in Creative mode:

- You can use the search screen in your inventory to find items.

- If you are destroying a large area of dirt or stone, for example, use a dirt or stone block to do it. This way, you can easily replace a space you didn't mean to make with the block in your hand.

- You can use your mouse middle key as a pick block. By middle-clicking a block, you place it in your hotbar and your hand.

- Empty buckets stay empty, and water and lava buckets stay filled.

- You have access to Creative mode–only blocks— the sponge block (decorative) and spawn eggs, which you place on the ground to spawn mobs like sheep or creepers.

- When it rains, use commands to stay in daylight and clear weather: Use **/weather clear 10000** to stop the rain for 10,000 seconds and **/time set day** to go back to daylight.

You can play a tune by tuning note blocks in a sequence and activating them through redstone power. You make a note block a half-note higher each time you right-click it. An un-clicked note block makes an F-sharp note, so to make it sound a G, click once. Once you reached the highest note possible (after two octaves), it returns to emitting the lowest note. You can change the tone of the sound by changing the block beneath the note block. Most blocks, including dirt, produce piano tones. Glass blocks produce clicks. Sand and gravel produce a snare drum sound. Wood blocks produce a bass guitar sound and stone blocks produce a bass drum sound.

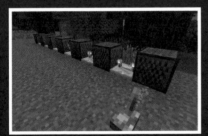

Connect tuned note blocks together with repeaters and activate to make a tune.

For example, the opening seven notes for "Twinkle Twinkle Little Star" are G, G, D, D, E, E, D. Set up seven note blocks in a row, with one repeater (pointing to the next note in sequence) between each. Right-click each repeater three times for the maximum signal delay. Then, tune each of the seven notes. For a G, right-click it once; for a D, right-click eight times; and for an E, right-click ten times. Power the first G note block with a lever and redstone wire. Flip the lever, and you'll get the tune!

jukebox in Minecraft you can craft with a d
e of eight wood planks. To find music disc
d to do some exploring, as only a couple of
n dungeon chests.

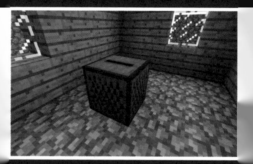

To get more music discs, you'll have to trick a skeleton
reeper. One way to do this is to first damage the creep
t, with three blows from a stone sword. This means th
can then kill it with one arrow. Lead the creeper until y
t into position between you and a skeleton. Then wall
keeping the creeper between you and the skeleton. Ar
first lure the skeleton into one end of a ditch and a dar
nto the other end.

If you can g
skeleton to
creeper, th
will drop a

# CHAPTER 15

## THE NETHER

The Nether is Minecraft's fiery underworld. There is no day or night, no flowers, ponds, or villagers—it is a dark world lit by lava and flames. The terrain is dangerous, with seas of lava and high, treacherous cliffs. The Nether is teeming with its own dangerous mobs: zombie pigmen, enormous firebombing ghasts, whirling blazes, shifty endermen, creepy magma cubes, and Wither skeletons.

The Nether landscape: columns and seas of lava, floating islands of Netherrack, raging fires, and plenty of dangerous mobs.

So why go there? It is only place you can find the rarest of Minecraft's materials. There is glowstone to make redstone lamps, Nether quartz to make redstone comparators and daylight sensors, and Nether wart for potions. The items dropped made by Nether mobs you kill are especially valuable. Magma cream and ghast tears are used for potions. So are blaze rods, which you also need to find to lead you to the End. And if you want to accomplish all of Minecraft's achievements, including getting to the End, you will need to visit and raid a Nether fortress.

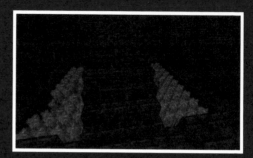

You can find Nether wart growing at the bottom of fortress staircases.

To visit the Nether, you must construct a portal of at least ten obsidian blocks surrounding a three-block-high, two-block-wide empty space. Once built, you activate the portal by igniting the center space with flint and steel or a fire charge.

You only need ten obsidian blocks to make a portal, but you can make portals as big as 23 × 23.

Stand in the portal to be teleported. When the animation stops, step out into the Nether. Watch out: a portal can spawn near or over lava, a tiny ledge suspended in midair, and other dangerous places. Secure your portals with a cobblestone wall to keep out the mobs on either side. Even better, create a roofed base of operations around your Nether portal. Cobblestone can withstand the fireballs that ghasts throw.

Make sure you are equipped at least with a full set of armor, as well as potions, enchanted weapons, and tools to help you survive and fight. You'll need your swords, bows, and pickaxe. You'll need plenty of cobblestone to make bridges across the lakes of lava, as well as gravel and a shovel for pillar jumping up and down cliffs. You can also take ladders to help you climb. Take material to build another portal in case yours is destroyed. As with mining, bring chests to store loot, wood to make a crafting table, and iron to make new weapons and tools. Don't forget food!

## Find the Fortress

Your main priority in the Nether is to find a Nether fortress, but it's difficult to see well in the dim light. To help, you can use a Potion of Night Vision or change your video settings in your game options to maximize the screen's brightness and the render distance. Look for flat, dark, tall areas of Nether fortress walls that are straight up and down instead of the jagged pro-files of cliffs. Nether fortresses can have long walkways and tall windows. They are placed along north/south lines, so one tactic is to just head either east or west to find one. Compasses don't work in the Nether, so use your F3 Debug screen to get your direction. Use torches or Jack o'Lanterns to mark your path.

You can recognize a Nether fortress by the vertical dark shapes in the distance.

Bring plenty of cobblestone to build bridges over lava.

Once you get to your Nether fortress, you have several main goals:

- Locate chests and their valuable loot.

- Find Nether wart that grows around the bottom of staircases.

- Find a blaze spawner so you can kill multiple blazes and get the blaze rods they drop.

## Fighting the Nether Mobs

**Blaze**

Use snowballs against a blaze, as they cause three points of damage each and can give you some time to get close and use your sword. Build a small barricade to hide behind, popping out to damage them as they get close.

It can be hard getting close to a blaze to kill it and dangerous to take time loading arrows. Try snowballs—they deal three points of damage—as you get close with your sword.

### Zombie Pigmen

Zombie pigmen are neutral unless you attack one. Then the pigman, and any pigmen nearby, will attack you as a horde if they can see you. Avoid fighting them, or, if you must, stay more than sixteen blocks away and shoot with your bow. They are not very clever, and a wall can hold them at bay. You can push them off a cliff without provoking them. Baby zombie pigmen are faster than the adults, so they are a bit more dangerous.

Zombie pigmen are neutral until attacked. If you attack one, though, a host of others will join to pursue you.

### Ghasts

You can use any tool to smack back a ghast's fireballs. You can influence the direction by using an arrow or snowball to hit the fireball. Move side to side to prevent the ghast from getting a good aim at you. Fire your arrows at their tentacles. One arrow from an enchanted bow can kill them. They only have ten health points, so if you can bring one close, you can kill it in one or two blows from a sword.

You can use any tool to smack back a ghast's fireball.

### Magma Cubes

Magma cubes are like slime but more dangerous. Use a bow to kill the big ones first and move back as it spawns smaller ones. Wait to use your sword on the small ones.

A magma cube is the Nether version of slime.

### Wither Skeletons

Keep your distance so you can use a bow and arrow. Because a Wither skeleton is over two blocks high, create a barricade with a 2 × 1 hole you can escape and fight through.

Wither skeletons are over two blocks high, so you can place barricades and doors that only you can pass through.

## More Nether Tips

- If you get completely lost, you can create another portal to take you back to the Overworld.

- Some mobs can travel through a portal, and items can be thrown through a portal. Storage mine-carts, powered minecarts, empty minecarts, and boats can also go through a portal.

- If you are bringing back Nether wart for growing, don't forget the Soul Sand it grows in. You can usually find Soul Sand near lava.

- One way to store your Nether loot is in an Ender chest. An Ender chest is an interdimensional chest, and wherever you build the chest you will have access to the same materials. So you can build an Ender chest in the Nether to hold your loot. To access the same loot from the Overworld, just build another Ender chest. An Ender chest is built with eight obsidian blocks and one Eye of Ender.

All of the contents you place in an Ender chest are available in any realm, wherever you place another Ender chest.

- Bring golden and enchanted golden apples. Either will help regenerate you, and an enchanted golden apple also provides fire resistance.

- Since your chances of dying in the Nether are high, leave very valuable items at home in a chest.

- Maps can help you in the Nether. Even though they don't show any landmarks, they do show you where you are in relationship to the center of the map, which is the point you first use the map. So if you start a map at your Nether portal, you will be able to see the direction you must go to get back there.

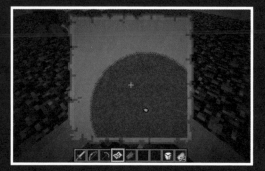

A map in the Nether only shows you the bedrock ceiling, but it will show you where you are from the map's center.

- Try to kill ghasts over land so you can gather their tears.

- Don't bring water or beds. Water will sizzle up so you can't use it, and trying to sleep in a bed will explode the bed.

- You can use a fishing rod to catch a ghast, bring it close over land, and attack with a sword.

## Portal Networks

Because traveling one block in the Nether is the same as traveling eight blocks in the Overworld, you can create a network of portals in the Nether that allow you to travel far distances in the Overworld. The most reliable way of doing this is creating the connected portals by hand. First you create the Overworld portal at coordinates x, y, and z. Then travel to the Nether and create a portal there that will bring you back to where you built the first portal in the Overworld. Do this by finding the spot with the coordinates x/8 (the value of x divided by 8), y, and z. The height axis, y, is matched as closely as possible in Overworld/Nether mapping. You may have to dig in the Netherrack, create bridges over lava, or create a platform to build your Nether portal on. In the Nether, you can create paths, stairs, and bridges between your Nether portals, along with signs so you can remember which portals lead where. This doesn't always work exactly as you plan, and a portal may end up in a different area than you expect. You may need to experiment as you go.

## More Portal Tips

- In Survival mode, you have about four seconds in the portal while you are being teleported. During this time, you can change your mind and step back into the Overworld.

- If you create a second portal close to another in the Overworld (within about 1,024 blocks in the Overworld), the second portal will transport you to the same Nether portal as the first. In the Nether, the distance to maintain separate portals is 128 blocks.

- You can create a portal without needing a diamond pickaxe to mine obsidian. Instead, you create the obsidian by creating waterfalls against a wall, then pouring lava from a bucket onto the blocks where the obsidian frame should be.

You can create a portal by making waterfalls and pouring lava onto the blocks where obsidian should be.

# CHAPTER 16
## THE END AND BEYOND

**A**lthough Minecraft is a sandbox game designed for endless exploration and play, it does have a victory to achieve called "The End." To finish the game and win, you have to go to the End, of course. The End is a special realm in the same way the Nether is. It is a series of islands, separated by about a thousand blocks, floating in the void, populated by Endermen and the Ender Dragon. Once there, your only task is to defeat the Ender Dragon, which is extremely difficult. If you defeat the dragon, Minecraft shows you the end credits along with a poem called "The End." Once you have defeated the dragon, she will leave behind a dragon egg and an End portal will appear that takes you to one of the surrounding islands. Use the egg to summon another dragon. Defeating additional dragons opens up to twenty new End portals that take you to different islands you can explore.

The End is a collection of islands floating in the void, where Endermen , shulkers, and the Ender Dragon live.

## Eyes of Ender

In order to get to the end and defeat the dragon, you must have Eyes of Ender. Eyes of Ender are used to find End portals that transport you to the End. End portals are found in underground structures called strongholds. However, the End portal is broken, and to repair it you will need up to twelve more Eyes of Ender. The highly prized Eyes of Ender are crafted by combining blaze powder with Ender pearls, or you may be able to trade for them with village priests. To find an End portal, throw the Eye of Ender in the air. Do this in an area where you have a good view. If you are far from the End portal, the eye will float off in the direction of the portal and drop so you can pick it up again. Repeat this action until the Eye of Ender drops straight onto the ground in front of you. (You may need three or four eyes to finish this task.) This means the End portal is below you. When you dig, create a spiraling staircase or a ladder shaft so you don't stray too far from the spot.

Throw an Eye of Ender and follow its direction to locate a stronghold.

## The End Portal

The End portal is in a room and is placed over a pool of lava. There is also a silverfish spawner you will need to destroy, along with any silverfish. Don't destroy any of the blocks the portal is created with, though—you can't replace them. Go ahead and add your Eyes of Ender to any of the portal blocks that are missing them. Once all eyes are in place, the portal will activate.

A stronghold's portal room contains a broken portal over a pool of lava and a silverfish spawner.

Fix and activate the portal by adding Eyes of Ender.

## Strongholds

Strongholds are pretty interesting places you should look for even if you don't care about the Ender Dragon. Each Minecraft world you create has a maximum of 128 strongholds. They are a maze of dungeon-like rooms. In addition to the End portal room, these include rooms with fountains, libraries with bookshelves, and storage rooms with chests. But beware of digging through the walls, as this can release and provoke silverfish hiding in blocks.

Strongholds are a maze of rooms that include libraries, storage rooms with chests, and fountain rooms.

## Preparing for the End

The only way to get back from the End is to win or be killed and respawn. Since you may need to try several times to kill the Ender Dragon, set up a base at the stronghold, sleeping in a bed so that if you are killed, you respawn there. That way you'll have everything you need (including enchanted bows and swords, food, blocks, etc.) to take another trip to the End. You may even want to plan on taking an exploratory trip to the End, to survey it and plan what you will need, then die to come back to your new spawn point in the End portal room.

You will want to take diamond and, if possible, enchanted armor and weapons. Bring at least two stacks of tipped arrows if you don't have an infinity enchantment. Use Sharpness enchantment for your sword and Feather Fall for your boots. Bring a pumpkin and helmet, gravel and a shovel for pillar jumping (or ladders), and a pickaxe for digging. Bring a stack of obsidian to build bridges that the dragon can't destroy.

## The End Itself

When you enter the End, you are deposited on a small island with columns of obsidian, hordes of Endermen, and the massive Ender Dragon. You will spawn on a ledge of obsidian, and the ledge may be some distance from the dragon's island. You may need to build or dig your way to the island.

## Defeating the Dragon

The dragon is a very powerful boss mob that can wipe out half of your health with one blow. It is called a boss mob because it is programmed with more complex actions and reactions than regular mobs. When it is near you, your display shows the dragon's health bar.

You can wear a pumpkin so you don't look at any Endermen by accident and provoke them. Next, locate the Ender crystals on towers. These help the dragon heal quickly, and you must destroy these. Use a bow and enchanted arrows to do this, because the crystals explode when they are destroyed. You may need to build a pillar to get high enough to destroy some crystals. Keep some distance from them or use enchanted diamond armor.

The crystals on top of obsidian columns repair the Ender Dragon's health. To defeat the dragon you must destroy these first.

To kill the dragon, wait until it is flying right at you, then aim your arrow at its head. This causes the most damage. With the pumpkin on your head, you only need to worry about the dragon. It may take some time to damage the dragon enough to kill it, so have plenty of arrows. When the dragon dies, it explodes. Beneath it is an exit portal with a dragon egg on top. Take the exit portal to view the end credits and poem and get back to your last spawn point in the Overworld!

Fire at the dragon's head to cause the most damage.

## More End Tips

- If you don't want to use a pumpkin to avoid Endermen, build an Iron Golem army to help kill Endermen.

- When you hit the dragon and do damage, it flies away for a little bit. You can use this time to regroup or run somewhere else.

- The Ender Dragon can topple cobblestone, so bring obsidian to build shelters and bridges.

- The dragon egg will spawn a new dragon and open an End portal as well as a gateway portal to a new island for you to explore. However, the egg is difficult to retrieve. One way is to first click on the egg with a tool to make it teleport a few blocks away. Then dig just one block out, two spaces below the egg. Place a torch in this space. Then knock out the block just below it to make the egg drop again as a resource. Now you can pick it up. To prevent the dragon egg initially teleporting into the exit portal, cover the exit portal with blocks temporarily.

- You can teleport with an Ender pearl, but it will cost you five points of damage. Throw the Ender pearl by right-clicking and you will teleport where it lands.

## Beyond the End

Once you reach the End, that's not it! Defeat the Wither, vanquish additional Ender Dragons, explore the Outer Islands and discover End cities to find even more treasures. And of course, there is no end to the games you can play, worlds you can visit, maps you can explore, and machines you can build. There's a vast community of miners ready with suggestions and tips for new ways to play and have fun.

## Outer End Islands

Once you defeat the Ender Dragon and your health and hunger are restored, throw an Ender pearl into a gateway portal to be teleported to an Outer End Island. While some Outer Islands are barren wastelands populated only by Endermen and chorus trees that you can harvest for their chorus fruit, others contain End cities which can be explored for valuable loot.

An End city is a rare, beautiful structure composed of purple purpur blocks, stairs, slabs, and columns, as well as End stone bricks. The cities can be small or large, often resemble castles, trees, or Japanese temples, and are lit only by End rods. Collect the building materials to build unique structures in the Overworld, but beware of shulkers, the shy creatures who lurk within the city walls. As you explore, keep an eye out for loot rooms that contain chests with valuable loot!

End cities often resemble castles, trees, or Japanese temples.

## Shulkers

The End cities are also home to shulkers, shy creatures that hide in a purpur block-like shell, teleport away when approached or damaged, and, most importantly, shoot sparks at you if you come too close. They only take damage when open and are best shot at from a distance to avoid being hit. Being hit by a spark causes you to levitate for ten seconds before being dropped to the ground, taking damage from the fall if you are unprotected. Removing blocks around the shulker, leaving it out in the open, will cause it

## End Ship

The rare End ship can be found floating near an End city. Throw an Ender pearl at the deck of the ship to teleport there. This small ship features a dragon head at the front that you can obtain. Bring the head back with you to the Overworld and power it with redstone to open and close its mouth. You'll also find a brewing stand with potions of Healing, a treasure room, and an item frame holding Elytra. Defeat the shulker guarding the treasure first to make looting easier.

## Elytra

Each End ship holds only one pair of Elytra. These wings form a gliding cape that you place in the chestplate slot. To use them, simply jump into the air and glide. Elytra will provide just over seven minutes of glide time, which can vary based on how you use them. Look left, right, up, or down to change direction as you fly. Elytra can be repaired by combining two damaged pairs with leather on an anvil or enchanted with Unbreaking or Mending.

## Create and Destroy a Wither

The Wither is a three-headed boss mob that can only be created by a player. To fill the achievement of spawning a Wither, you must first kill the Ender Dragon. To build a Wither, you must stack Soul Sand in a T, similar to making a golem. Then you place three wither skeleton skulls on the top of the T. When the Wither is spawned, it flashes, grows, and creates a large explosion. Run away as soon as you create the Wither to avoid being damaged or killed. You will want to be using enchanted diamond armor and weapons, as well as potions. To fight the Wither, use bows as you approach, then drink a strength potion and use your enchanted diamond sword to kill it at close range.

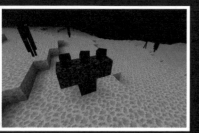

Right after you create a Wither, it flashes, then explodes, before enlarging to its final shape.

One tactic that some players use to defeat the Wither is to create a small room at the top of the Nether, with bedrock as its ceiling. Here you can create the Wither on a piston and activate the piston to raise the Wither's heads into the bedrock. Once the Wither has exploded, it is still stuck in the bedrock, and you can kill it with your sword. Because the Wither creates so much damage by hurling exploding Wither skulls, you might want to fight it in the End, after you've defeated the dragon, of course.

Beacons are blocks that shoot up columns of light and can be powered to give you special powers. To build a beacon you must have a Nether star, which is dropped when you kill the Wither. It is therefore one of the rarest Minecraft blocks. It must be built on a pyramid of iron, gold, emerald, or diamond blocks (not ore). The smallest base it can be built on (level 1) is a 3 × 3 block, and the largest it can be built on is a 9 × 9 base pyramid (level 4).

There are four sizes of beacon you can make, using gold, emerald, iron, and diamond blocks. Larger beacons deliver more powerful effects.

Beacons are great for making a visible landmark. Even better, you can add an iron or gold ingot or an emerald or diamond to it to gain special powers, some of which are the same as abilities given by potions. The special powers are haste, speed, jump boost, strength, resistance, and regeneration. The special powers only affect you if you are within a certain distance of the beacon: within twenty blocks of a level 1 beacon, going up to fifty blocks for level 4. Each level gives you increasing choices of powers that can be granted. Level 1 beacons only offer speed and haste, while Level 4 beacons can give you two powers at the same time. Once you've built a beacon, right-click it to access its activation screen to add the iron, gold, emerald, or diamond and activate its powers.

Yes, there's even more to do! Although you can play endlessly in singleplayer mode, you can also play user-created maps and try multiplayer Minecraft. To play multiplayer you will need access to a server, or you will need a home network to set up your own server. If you are joining a server you will need to understand the risks and requirements involved in this. It's best to have an experienced friend or parent show you the ropes, both with joining a server or with setting up a server for you and your friends to play on. In multiplayer, you can chat with other players and form groups to build amazing cities, houses, and castles, or just survive together. An easier way to set up a multiplayer world is through Minecraft Realms. This is a Mojang service that lets you set up an online world and share it with other players, but it does require a monthly fee.

You can also play specially created maps that are built by other users to test your abilities. Many maps can be played in singleplayer mode. Some maps use game mods (modification applications). You need to be sure you are running the same version of the game that the map uses, as well as any mods needed.

There are several types of maps you can play. Adventure maps give you a quest to perform and survival maps are designed to test your fighting and survival skills. There are also puzzle maps, which give you logical puzzles to solve, and parkour maps. Parkour maps test your agility running and jumping between platforms, columns, and ledges. There are also creative maps, which have amazing and creative builds for you to enjoy. Once you've played lots of maps, you may have your own idea for a map to create!

**Caution**
It is pretty easy to mess up your version of Minecraft—even your computer—when you download and install unofficial files

like mods and maps, so it is best to have someone experienced with this read through the instructions and help you, make sure your current games are backed up, and help re-install Minecraft if there's a problem.